Harley-Davidson
Collectibles

Photographs by Nick Cedar
Text by Michael Dregni

TOWN
SQUARE
BOOKS

an imprint of Voyageur Press

Edited by Todd R. Berger
Designed by Andrea Rud
Printed in Hong Kong

98   99   00   01   02   5   4   3   2   1

Library of Congress Cataloging-in-Publication Data
Dregni, Michael, 1961–
        Harley-Davidson collectibles / photographs by Nick Cedar ; text by Michael Dregni.
            p.   cm.
        "A Town Square book."
        Includes bibliographical references and index.
        ISBN 0-89658-367-8
        1. Harley-Davidson motorcycle—Collectibles.   2. Harley-Davidson motorcycle—Parts—Collectors and collecting.   I. Title.
        TL448.H3D74 1998
        629.227'5—dc21   97-44769
                                    CIP

A Town Square Book
Published by Voyageur Press, Inc.
123 North Second Street, P.O. Box 338, Stillwater, MN 55082 U.S.A.
612-430-2210, fax 612-430-2211

Educators, fundraisers, premium and gift buyers, publicists, and marketing managers: Looking for creative products and new sales ideas? Voyageur Press books are available at special discounts when purchased in quantities, and special editions can be created to your specifications. For details contact the marketing department at 800-888-9653.

Page 1: Miscellaneous Harley-Davidson and general motorcycling memorabilia from the 1950s. *Ron Sabie collection.*
Page 2: Miscellaneous Harley-Davidson and general motorcycling memorabilia from the 1950s. *Ron Sabie collection.*
Page 3: A cast-iron Harley-Davidson toy from the 1930s made by Hubley. *Doug Leikala collection.*
Page 6: Miscellaneous Harley-Davidson and general motorcycling memorabilia from the 1980s. *Dudley Perkins Harley-Davidson collection.*

Acknowledgments

In creating the images for this book, we had the pleasure of meeting and exploring the collections of some of the most devoted enthusiasts in the country. Without the substantial investment of time and personal resources of these people, the memories preserved by their dedication would be gone forever. Just one small sampling of fobs or matchbooks can represent thousands of miles traveled and hours spent combing swap meets and stores. Call it obsession or call it passion, but what lies on the shelves and in the drawers and cabinets of the collections featured in this book can only be described as labors of love.

One of the first collectors to really show us the potential of the subject was Chris Haynes. Chris not only has an outstanding collection and an encyclopedia-like knowledge of Harley-Davidson, but is also as generous with his valuable time as he is with his information. Karla and George Threedouble, who have devoted substantial time, money, and space to their fantastic collection, were also supportive and provided crucial material and information. Paul Wheeler and Mike Parti have quietly assembled fine collections of their own, with one-of-a-kind items that add immeasurably to these pages. Vince Spadaro and Tom Perkins have both taken time away from running busy shops to help us photograph their excellent collections of motorcycling history. Doug Leikala's devotion to keeping the mementos of the past preserved and displayed in his collection rivals the efforts of many small museums. Doug has methodically put together items that represent the true heart of motorcycling's birth in America. His enthusiasm for this project, like that of the others, was invaluable.

All of these collectors selflessly devoted rare free days, often on weekends, to help us document their efforts. As they continue to comb the land for the bits of history that they covet, the fans of American motorcycling owe them a debt of gratitude for holding onto and sharing the items that helped shape a company and a nation of enthusiasts.

Thanks in addition are due to the following people, listed in alphabetical order, who helped with various other aspects of the book: Eric Dregni, for information on traffic laws of the early years of the Motor Age; Greg Field, author of two excellent histories of Harley-Davidson models, *Harley-Davidson Panheads* and *Harley-Davidson Knuckleheads*, for his assistance; Tim Gartman, for information on printing processes and graphic styles of early sales literature; Ken Giannini of the Minnesota State Fair for supplying photographs of motorcycle racing; Patty Marino of Fender Musical Instruments, Scottsdale, Arizona, for supplying the photograph of the Fender Harley-Davidson Stratocaster; the Minnesota Historical Society for supplying photographs of early Harley-Davidson dealerships; and Lloyd L. Rich.

Thanks as well to the owners of the motorcycles pictured in this book, listed here in alphabetical order: Gary Aguirre, Ron Blackford, Ray Ebersole, Armando Magri, Rick Najera, David Patrick, Mike Quinn, Russ Sierck, and John Van Dyke.

Finally, Mike Parti put into words the sentiment that we think is shared by all collectors, that he is not the owner of these items, but merely a caretaker of future memories.

Thank you all.

Nick Cedar
Michael Dregni

Contents

The Value *of* Harley-Davidson Collectibles

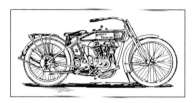

As time goes by, all we have of the past are memories, photographs, and mementos. Sadly, our memories can be fleeting; what seemed so important in the present can be lost to the future. It is often left to photographs and mementos to hold the key to our own history, to serve a valuable role as mnemonics, evoking the past, telling stories, and reminding us of where we have been, people we have met, and good times we have had.

These mnemonics take on more importance as life moves on. A 1960s Harley-Davidson general catalog, faded with age and dog-eared with use, may remind you of your own childhood perusing the model details and specifications with a long-lost buddy. An old riding cap, purchased through the Harley-Davidson accessory catalog in the 1930s and once the height of fashion, may have been cast aside decades ago only to be rediscovered, crumpled and dust covered, but still a reminder of sunny days and the road unrolling beneath your motorcycle.

These photographs and mementos are also artifacts of our collective motorcycling history with larger tales to tell. The leather motorcycle "helmets" of the 1920s—modeled on aviator caps and football gear—remind us of the riding conditions of that era when most roads were not paved and speeds were a fraction of what they are today, making such a "helmet" a passable crash lid for the time and not as ridiculous as it may appear from our modern vantage point. A poster heralding a

Harley-Davidson memorabilia, 1910s and 1920s
Facing page: The motorcycling world of the 1900s, 1910s, and 1920s witnessed some rapid advances in technical development—both revolutionary and evolutionary—all at the same time. Mementos of the era provide a window into motorcycling lore of the day. *Ron Sabie and Russ Sierck collections.*

motordrome race of the 1910s brings forth images of the long-lost days of the pine-board motordromes—perhaps the most thrilling yet bloody era of motorcycle sports—and makes at least a part of those races live again in our imagination.

This is a book of photographs and mementos, and, ultimately, it is a book of Harley-Davidson nostalgia. It is a sentimental look at the olden days of motorcycling, when our Harley-Davidsons were new, beckoning from the showroom floor in all their chromed finery—or at least new to us, well-ridden, well-used, and well-worn, but still great machines. It is also a look back at the way we were, at motorcycling fashions that were once high style but today seem whimsical and enchanting, mechanical advances that seemed like rocket science then but appear quaint now, and fads that once swept the globe by storm but are joked about today. In this light, these mnemonics take on great historical and sociological value by opening a window to days gone by.

There are, unfortunately, limits to how many Harley-Davidson motorcycles one person can own, limits imposed by money, garage space, restoration time, and by the simple physical fact that one person can only ride one motorcycle at a time. But there are no limits to the number of photographs and mementos—and ultimately, memories—a person can collect. There are few Harley-Davidson enthusiasts who do not have at least one motorcycling memento that is valuable to them.

As a word of warning, this book is not a memorabilia collector's price guide. Prices for collectibles and antiques tend to be out of date as soon as they see print. Prices are also extremely variable, and at the same time, personal: Certain collectibles may command thousands of dollars at auction, whereas the simple enameled metal pin you may have been awarded for participating in the 1952 Gypsy Tour may be priceless to you.

As a second warning, this is not a complete identification guide to Harley-Davidson memorabilia either. Such a guide could never be assembled. Happily, the artifacts shown in this book are only the tip of the iceberg.

Instead, it's our intention that this book be a celebration of times past in our pastime, a history of motorcycling lore told from a different vantage point, told with photographs and text describing another side of the world of Harley-Davidson. If this book resurrects some memories—and awakens some ghosts—then it is a success.

Evel Knievel souvenir program, 1971
Left: Aboard his XR-750, Robert "Evel" Knievel was one of the colorful, charismatic, and slightly crazy heroes of the 1970s motorcycling world. He earned his legendary status by jumping his motorcycle over just about anything that was in his way, from the Snake River of Wyoming to the fountain pool at Caesar's Palace in Las Vegas. No one who witnessed his exploits could fail to be moved—in some way or another. *Doug Leikala collection.*

Harley-Davidson memorabilia, 1930s
Facing page: It was the best of times and the worst of times. With motorcycle sales down during the Great Depression, the Motor Company had to fight tooth and nail in the 1930s with rival Indian for wins on the racetracks and sales on the showroom floors. In 1935, Harley-Davidson finally unveiled its secret weapon, the overhead-valve Series E Knucklehead, but the new machine went back under wraps and was not sold until 1936, and then only in limited numbers. Still, the overhead-valve engine would become the company's savior. *Ron Sabie and Russ Sierck collections.*

Fender Harley-Davidson Stratocaster, 1993

Left: The Fender Stratocaster is to electric guitars what Harley-Davidson is to motorcycles: an American icon. It's only natural that rock and roll and motorcycles should go together, so in 1993, the Fender Musical Instruments Corporation of Scottsdale, Arizona, created a limited-edition Stratocaster, in cooperation with Harley-Davidson, commemorating the Motor Company's ninetieth anniversary. This Strat featured an aluminum body and pickguard with hardware plated in chrome and gold. The maple neck, ebony fretboard, and stainless-steel frets were highlighted by an engraved plaque at the twelfth fret. Fender's famed Custom Shop built only 109 of these Strats, and the asking price often rivals that of a Big Twin. In 1995, Gibson USA also offered an acoustic guitar made at its former Bozeman, Montana, plant that bore the Harley-Davidson name in mother-of-pearl. The Gibson was limited to 1,500 examples. *Photograph by Pitkin Studio, courtesy of the Fender Musical Instruments Corp.*

Harley-Davidson memorabilia, 1970s

Below: The 1970s were tough years for the Motor Company, as the firm sought to establish its identity amid the turmoil of the decade. The firm was bought in 1969 and owned until 1981 by American Machine and Foundry (AMF), famous for its bowling balls and other sporting goods. *Dudley Perkins Harley-Davidson collection.*

Chapter 1

Selling Harley-Davidson

Sales Literature, Promotional Items, & Dealer Collectibles

It was the motorcycles themselves that first inspired us. Perhaps it was the sight of one of the pioneering Silent Gray Fellows motoring along a cobblestone city street at a speed you never thought imaginable in the days of horses and buggies. Or maybe it was a brand-spanking-new 1936 EL, resplendent with its marvelous overhead-valve engine that would prove to be the savior of the Harley-Davidson Motor Company. Or perhaps it was a Glide, blue and white two-tone like Elvis Presley's in his 1967 flick *Clambake*, seen here in real life, parked at the curb, a glorious sight in chrome, dressed up with the gigantic speedometer on the mile-wide gas tank, a fluted airhorn, windshield, and rhinestone-encrusted leather saddlebags emblazoned with the name "Tex."

In the early days of motorcycling, back when the first motorized bicycles were as rare as hen's teeth, back before motorcycles had any sort of bad image beyond scaring the occasional horse, you rode the streetcar downtown to the city bicycle shop that had just made a big step into the future and ordered an early Harley-Davidson. This strange beast stood there on the showroom floor, a gleaming vision of tomorrow amongst the suddenly old-fashioned pedal bicycles that were quickly pushed to the back of the shop.

Selling Harley-Davidson
Facing page: Harley-Davidson made an art of selling motorcycles by providing dealers with a plethora of promotional items, sales information, posters, and more—all bearing the company's logo. Many dealers also ordered their own promotional items independently of the Motor Company, including everything from giveaway pencils to ashtrays. For identification of the pictured items, see page 16. *Doug Leikala collection.*

In the 1930s, you may have run across an ad for Harley-Davidson in the back pages of *Popular Mechanics* or some other boffin journal, sent a postcard to an address in faraway Milwaukee and, miraculously, a catalog appeared in your mailbox, leaving you to spend days poring over the pictures until the pages turned ragged.

In the 1960s, you didn't dare even mention the name Harley-Davidson around your parents or other polite company, but rolled up the glossy catalog underneath your baseball jacket and went to the tree fort to examine the specifications with your buddies in sworn secrecy.

The Motor Company worked hard at fostering that devotion for its machines. The sales brochure was often the first, and thus most important, item you saw. From the early flyers with their dramatic futuristic graphics to the sleek brochures of the 1990s with stylish photography, the sales literature was designed to lure you into Harley-Davidson's vast network of dealerships.

Entering a dealer's showroom was like walking into a candy store. Under the neon-lit Harley-Davidson sign, you opened the door to another world with gleaming new motorcycles lined up along the floor. Salespeople were ready with the latest specifications on the tips of their tongues. Posters explained motorcycle payment plans that came complete with penny banks and passbooks to help you save for your machine.

And when it was time to leave, the salesperson shook your hand and gave you a promotional keepsake imprinted with Harley-Davidson's shield emblem and the dealer's name and address: Thousands of pencils and pens, key fobs, matchbooks, and more were given away over the years to help enthusiasts remember where they saw that new cycle and to deter them from buying the wares of that other great American motorcycle manufacturer, the archrival Indian.

Sales memorabilia
Identification of the sales collectibles sampling on page 14:
1. *Accessory News* dealer information sheet from 1935 detailing new paint and decal schemes; 2. Desktop calendar, 1954; 3. 1931 letter from Harley-Davidson to Eiler's Cycle Shop in Meadville, Pennsylvania; 4. Pen and pencil set, 1950s; 5. Dealer name tag, 1960s; 6. Dealer decals from the 1940s and 1950s that were affixed to cycles sold through the shops; 7. Dealer business card, 1960s; 8. Dealer giveaway pin from the 1910s and Harley-Davidson national dealers sales conference pin from 1952; 9. Promotional brochure, 1910s; 10. National dealer convention souvenir, 1971; 11. Savings plan brochure and passbooks, 1930s and 1950s; 12. Kilbourn Estimator from the 1950s for estimating monthly payments; 13. Hang tags from the 1950s through the 1960s that told prospective buyers the model name and price.

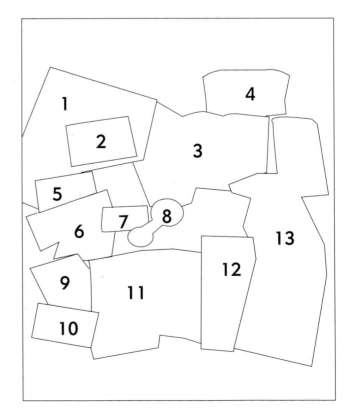

Harley-Davidson ad, 1909

Left: The Motor Company eschewed racing during its first decade, but when none other than Walter Davidson himself won a Diamond Medal at the 1908 Federation of American Motorcyclist (FAM) endurance and reliability contest in the Catskill Mountains of New York with a perfect score on his single-cylinder Harley-Davidson, the firm was happy to promote the win. This magazine ad asked would-be enthusiasts to send for a catalog, a common invitation in Harley-Davidson ads throughout the years. By simply addressing your letter or postcard to "Harley-Davidson Motor Company, Milwaukee," you could be assured that it would be delivered.

Sales literature, 1916 and 1927

Below: Enthusiasts spent untold hours poring over the Motor Company's sales catalogs and brochures, reading and re-reading the often flowery, purple prose; comparing specifications; and analyzing model details. With quaint and charming graphic images gracing their covers, these two Harley-Davidson brochures are typical of the firm's general catalogs during the first three decades. These catalogs showcase the 1916 (left) and 1927 lines. *Chris Haynes collection.*

Sales literature, 1920s

Above: An array of 1920s literature summarizing the sales process. The postcard was designed to lure prospective buyers to stop by their local dealership to "celebrate the arrival of springtime," and dealers would hand out copies of the latest model line brochure, like this 1928 catalog. When the sale was made, each owner was supplied with a rider's handbook, giving instructions on care and maintenance of their new motorcycle. Also available was the accessory catalog, such as this 1928 example, offering "Inspected & Approved" Harley-Davidson items encompassing everything from the period rider's clothing to optional dresser parts to personalize your mount. *Chris Haynes collection.*

1915 V-twin with sidecar

Left: Harley-Davidson made its name with its famous V-twin engines, but the Motor Company got its start in 1903 with vertical single-cylinder motors. It was not until 1909 that Harley and the Davidsons offered a V-twin—and that model was not offered again until 1911. This 1915 V-twin was powered by a 61-cubic-inch (1,000-cc) engine. Sidecars proved a popular alternative to the cars of the day, at least until the arrival of Henry Ford's inexpensive Model T. Owner: Russ Sierck.

Sales postcards

The Motor Company supplied postcards to dealers, who mailed the cards to lure prospective buyers into the showroom to view the latest models, as with these 1939 and 1940 cards (above). The same sales tactic was still in use in the 1960s (left), but the look of the postcards had changed dramatically. *Doug Leikala collection.*

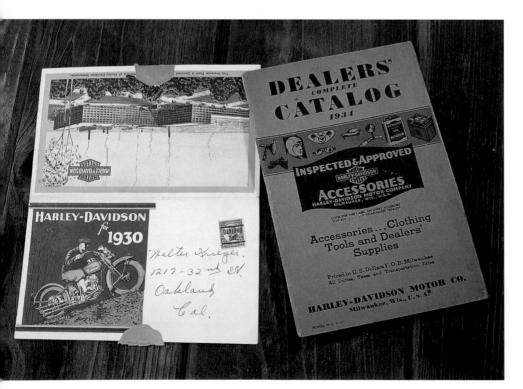

Sales literature, 1930s

Harley-Davidson's sales literature in the 1930s featured a new stylish look with multicolored, dramatic, graphic images depicting motorcycle scenes, details of the new models, and often boastful views of the Milwaukee factory, as with this 1930 brochure (left). These new styles of graphic design were in part made possibly by advances in commercial lithographic printing, and many dazzling brochures and posters were created by sales forces from Milwaukee to Hollywood. The 1934 Dealers' Complete Catalog of accessories (right) was much more business-like in its style. *Chris Haynes collection.*

"Fun All the Way," 1939

Advertisements in the back pages of large-circulation boffin magazines such as *Popular Mechanics* were the perfect medium to reach would-be enthusiasts in the early days of motorcycling. All you had to do was mail the coupon to Milwaukee, and a brochure and copy of Harley-Davidson's owner magazine, *The Enthusiast*, would be on the way.

Sales literature

By the late 1930s, Harley-Davidson's marketing force eschewed the dramatic graphic design of its earlier brochures and used state-of-the-art photo-process lithography to reproduce photographs of its latest motorcycles in catalogs, as with this 1940 brochure (right). The Motor Company's ad designers may have believed that the new, modern look of the brochures provided a more accurate representation of the company's wares, and the style was certainly in step with automobile manufacturers and the rival Indian motorcycle company. While these brochures have their own period charm, the days of the grand old illustrated sales catalogs were history. The 1954 accessory catalog (left) retained the straightforward style of its predecessors. *Chris Haynes collection.*

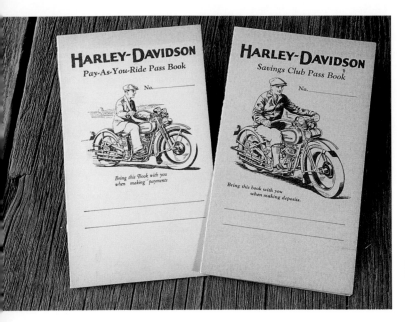

Payment plan poster, 1930s

Below: "It's easy to get your Harley-Davidson on these convenient plans . . ." announced this late-1930s poster, which once hung on a showroom wall. The Motor Company offered both its Savings Purchase and Pay-As-You-Ride plans to potential buyers. *Vince Spadaro collection.*

Savings passbooks, 1929–1930

Above: To help buyers save for their motorcycle through one of the firm's two payment plans, Harley-Davidson issued passbooks, such as these from 1929–1930. The ledger notebooks were modeled after bank books of the time, and aided buyers in keeping an account of their savings progress. *Doug Leikala collection.*

Savings bank, 1940s

Left: Harley-Davidson even offered a savings bank in the 1940s to speed along the day when the enthusiast would have enough nickels and dimes saved to buy a new Big Twin. If saving coins to buy a motorcycle seems far-fetched in this day and age, just remember that in 1940, a 74 UL Twin sold for a mere $385. This bank even had a plated motorcyclist on top as a constant reminder for the saver to remain conscientious. *Doug Leikala collection.*

Topper postcard, 1960
Topper aficionado Ed "Kookie" Byrnes was the heartthrob star of TV's *77 Sunset Strip*. *Michael & Eric Dregni collection.*

Topper motorscooter ad, 1960
Hoping to cash in on the motorscooter craze lead by the American Cushman and Italian Vespa scooters, Harley-Davidson released its Topper model in 1960 to fanfare boasting that it was "Tops in beauty and tops in performance." Unfortunately, the Topper never topped the sales records, and by 1965 was but a memory. *Michael & Eric Dregni collection.*

3-D sales viewer, 1960s
To promote its debut in the motor-scooter world in 1960, Harley-Davidson issued dealers a 3-D viewer that showed the new Topper in all of its two-toned, fiberglass glory. The Topper was the Motor Company's effort to cash in on the blossoming youth market for scooters, but against the all-conquering Piaggio Vespa and Cushman companies, even this viewer could not help Harley-Davidson win sales. The Motor Company made a quick exit from the scooter market. *Doug Leikala collection.*

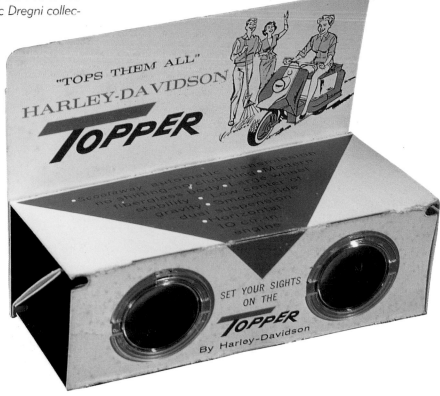

Dealership, 1900s

Many a bicycle shop jumped on the motorcycling bandwagon in the early 1900s as the pioneering "motorized bicycle" won converts among the speed-crazed and the newly mechanical-minded. This bicycle cum Harley-Davidson shop was run by Guy Webb in Minneapolis, Minnesota, and obviously he had just added the motorcycle line as the board painted with the words "Harley-Davidson" was simply nailed to the storefront—with a horseshoe hanging from the board for good luck in the novel venture. At that time, the horseshoe was a wise precaution, as a dealer probably approached such a bold, new enterprise with trepidation. *Minnesota Historical Society collection.*

Dealer sign, 1930s

Harley-Davidson offered advertising signs to its dealers to crown their showroom facades. The signs were typically made of metal with baked-on enamel paint; some included neon lights, such as this dealer sign from the 1930s. *Vince Spadaro collection.*

Dealer sign, 1930s

Below: A personalized dealer sign from the 1930s promising sales and service at Harley-Davidson St. Paul Co., of St. Paul, Minnesota. *Vince Spadaro collection.*

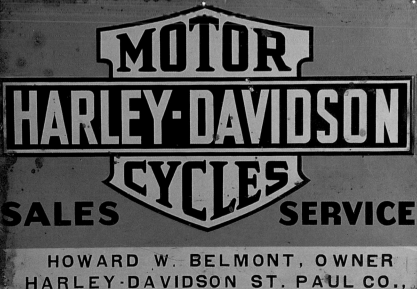

Dealer sign
A dealer sign that was to be mounted at a right angle on a dealership wall. *Chris Haynes collection.*

Dealership showroom, 1929
Above: Portrait of a typical Harley-Davidson dealership in the 1920s. The showroom is sparse of much advertising, except for the handful of Harley-Davidson promotional posters on the dividing wall. The two V-twins featured commercial-body sidecars, the one on the left painted with the legend, "Commercial Photographers/Special Delivery"; the one on the right for a dry cleaner's shop. *Minnesota Historical Society collection.*

Dealer sign, 1950s
With the availability of inexpensive plastics, backlit plastic dealer signs became the norm, as with this sign from the 1950s. Gone were the days of the glorious enameled-metal signs and their glowing neon—only to be revived in the 1990s with retro-styled signage. *Vince Spadaro collection.*

1930s Dealer sign
Above: A dealer sign ringed with orange neon. *Vince Spadaro collection.*

Promotional sign, 1965
Right: A 1965 promotional sign announced the updated Electra-Glide. *Chris Haynes collection.*

Complete New Styling!

'65 ELECTRA-GLIDE

- NEW FRONT CHAIN GUARD
- NEW GEAR CASE STYLING
- TURNPIKE TANKS
- NEW- DESIGN OIL TANK
- ALL-NEW ELECTRICAL SYSTEM

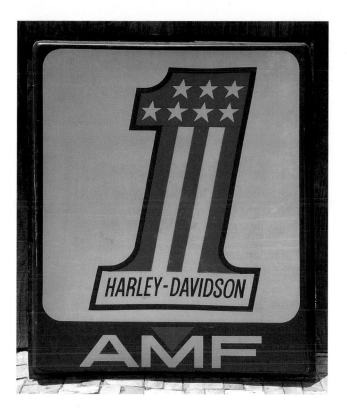

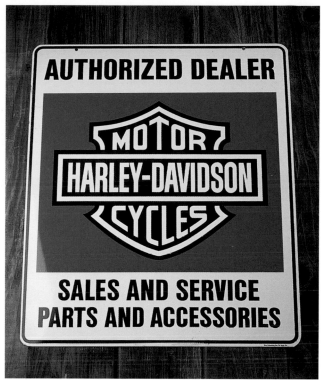

Dealer sign, 1970s

Above: In keeping with the fascination with the American stars and stripes in the 1970s, Harley-Davidson's ubiquitous "number one" logo, as shown on this 1970s dealer sign, fit the decade well. It also promoted the company's all-American image and the slogan "The Great American Freedom Machine" at a time when the image of the United States was tarnished by the Vietnam War. The Motor Company was purchased in 1969 and owned until 1981 by American Machine and Foundry (AMF). *Chris Haynes collection.*

Dealer sign, 1980s

The Motor Company returned to a simpler graphic design in the 1980s to promote itself, as on this enameled-metal dealer sign. The new image relied on the famous shield logo and the firm's colors of black and orange. *Chris Haynes collection.*

Dealer banner, 1985

Retro styling has infused Harley-Davidson's nostalgic character since the 1980s, as with this hanging showroom banner from 1985. *Threedouble collection.*

FULL LINE FUN LINE... FOR YOU!

→ the New '65 HARLEY-DAVIDSONS

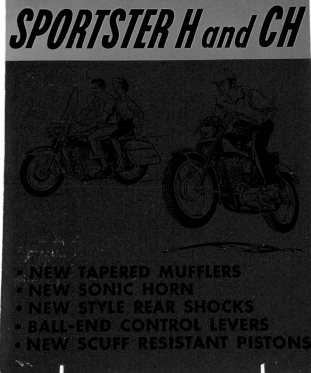

the lively ones for '65

SPORTSTER H and CH

- NEW TAPERED MUFFLERS
- NEW SONIC HORN
- NEW STYLE REAR SHOCKS
- BALL-END CONTROL LEVERS
- NEW SCUFF RESISTANT PISTONS

Promotional signs, 1965
Above, both photos: To announce the arrival of the new model year's lineup, Harley-Davidson issued promotional signs and posters to dealers, such as this sign heralding the "Full Line/Fun Line" of 1965 motorcycles and the Sportster H and CH models. *Chris Haynes collection.*

1966 FLH

The dressed Electra-Glide of the 1960s and 1970s became symbolic of all that was great about Harley-Davidson in those difficult decades. This FLH was powered by the 60-hp high-compression engine that displaced 74 cubic inches (1,200 cc). Dressed with the highway package, the Electra-Glide was the perfect American cruiser for the open road. Owner: Mike Quinn.

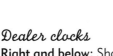

Dealer calendar, 1970s

Left: Calendars have long been used as a promotional sales tool by companies from Coca-Cola to Snap-On tools. Some calendars have featured cheesecake pictures, such as the famous Varga girls; others have featured pin-up motorcycles. This pocket calendar from the 1970s from Buffalo Harley-Davidson in Buffalo, New York, shows everyone's favorite Big Twin. *Doug Leikala collection.*

Dealer clocks

Right and below: Showroom clocks emblazoned with the company's logo have long been an advertising tool, catching people's eye with yet another sales pitch as they look at the time. These Harley-Davidson clocks are made of backlit plastic and date from the 1960s (below) and the 1980s. *Vince Spadaro collection (1960s clock) and Chris Haynes collection (1980s clock).*

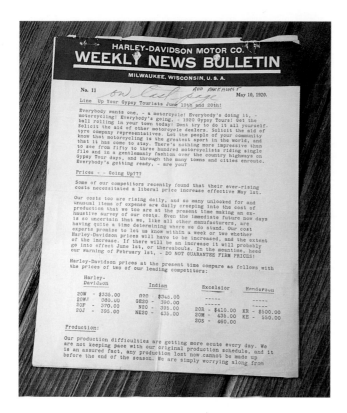

Dealer newsletter, 1920

Harley-Davidson issued newsletters to dealers, such as this Weekly News Bulletin from May 10, 1920, that were not meant for prying eyes. This bulletin admonishes dealers to heed the corporate warning not to guarantee firm prices to buyers, as a price increase from the then-current $335 for a 20W model was foreseen on the horizon. The current prices were also compared favorably against archrivals Indian, Excelsior, and Henderson to comfort dealers that Milwaukee prices were still the best. This dealer sheet was the property of legendary Harley-Davidson racer Leslie "Red" Parkhurst, originally of Denver, Colorado. *Mike Parti collection.*

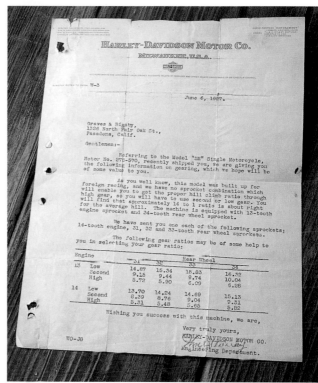

Dealer letter, 1927

Dealers often had direct access to the Motor Company's best and brightest racing and development engineers, as proven by this letter of June 6, 1927, from William "Bill" Ottaway in the Engineering Department. Ottaway first won fame as the head of the Thor motorcycle racing team and went on to become a legendary Harley-Davidson racer and race engineer. His letter in response to a query from the Graves & Bigsby dealership in Pasadena, California, provided detailed gearing ratios for hill climbing with a rare Model SM single, originally built for "foreign racing," as Ottaway notes. *Mike Parti collection.*

Transistor radios, 1970s

Transistor radios modeled after Harley-Davidson oil cans from the 1970s. These radios were offered through the Motor Company catalog. *Chris Haynes collection.*

1941 FL

There was great jubilation when the 61 OHV Knucklehead was first shown to Harley-Davidson dealers at the annual dealers convention on November 25, 1935. Here was the overhead-valve engine that the Motor Company and its dealers believed would bring them up to date and pull them out of the sales slump brought on by the Great Depression and the war with Indian. But the 61 OHV was not ready for production at the time, and it would be several months before dealers actually had Knuckleheads in their showrooms. But Harley-Davidson and its dealers were right on one count: The overhead-valve would save the day for the Motor Company, evolving into the Panhead and Shovelhead, and becoming the foundation on which the Evolution engine was built. Owner: Armando Magri.

Worker union pin, 1945
The Motor Company has been a union shop since 1937. This 1945 pin was worn by a Harley Davidson worker who was a member of the United Auto Workers (UAW) union. *Doug Leikala collection.*

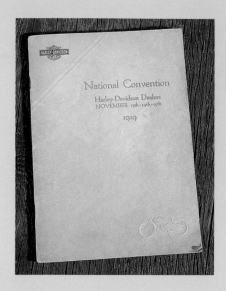

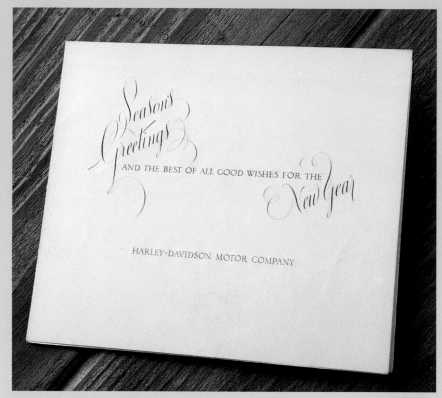

Dealer convention program, 1919

Above: Harley-Davidson officials and dealers met each year at a convention to unveil the new models, discuss problems, and plot against Indian. This program is from the November 13–15, 1919, national convention. *Dudley Perkins Harley-Davidson collection.*

Christmas greetings, 1920

Right, both photos: Harley-Davidson sent its 1920 Christmas greetings and best wishes for the New Year to its loyal league of dealers. This card was signed by Motor Company executives, including William H., Gordon, Walter and Arthur Davidson, William J. Harley, William Ottaway, and others. This particular card was sent to legendary racer Red Parkhurst. *Mike Parti collection.*

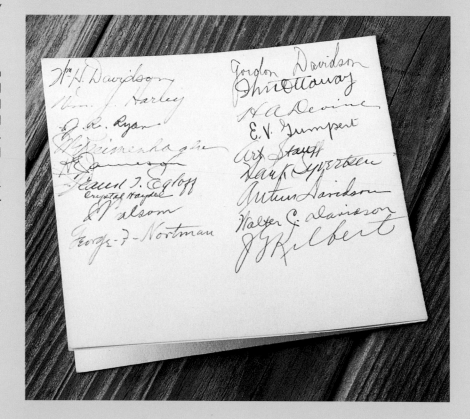

Promotional penguin, 1970s
Above: A stuffed penguin mascot featuring the Harley-Davidson "number one" logo from the 1970s. This penguin was offered through the Motor Company catalog. *Chris Haynes collection.*

Beer stein, 1983
Left: The Motor Company offered this commemorative beer stein in 1983. This style of stein was one of the earliest produced. *Threedouble collection.*

Promotional pens and pencils

Above: A selection of Harley-Davidson dealer giveaway pens and pencils from the 1960s through the 1990s. *Dudley Perkins Harley-Davidson collection.*

Promotions

Facing page and left: Identification: 1. Savings banks, 1950s and 1960s; 2. Dealership postcard, 1950s; 3. Topper scooter postcard featuring Ed "Kookie" Burns of TV's *77 Sunset Strip*, 1960s; 4. Ice scraper, 1960s; 5. "Blow Your Mind" whistle, 1970s; 6. Lighters, 1950s and 1960s; 7. Coin purse, 1957; 8. Belt buckle, 1950s; 9. Pin, 1970s; 10. Pocket knife, 1960s; 11. Poker chips, 1930s; 12. Matchbooks, 1930s through 1950s; 13. Measuring tape, 1970s; 14. Key chains, 1950s and 1970s; 15. Clip, 1960s; 16. New model postcards, 1960s; 17. Souvenir coin, 1950s; 18. Bottle opener, 1930s; 19. Bottle opener, 1956; 20. Pocket watch fobs, 1940s and 1950s; 21. Screwdriver, 1950s; 22. Bottle opener, 1960s; 23. Ruler, 1950s; 24. Key case, 1940s; 25. Horseshoe puzzle, 1920s; 26. Box opener, 1920s; 27. Lapel pin, 1950s. *Doug Leikala collection.*

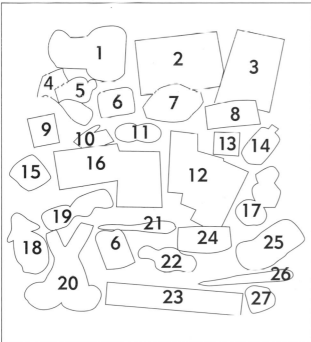

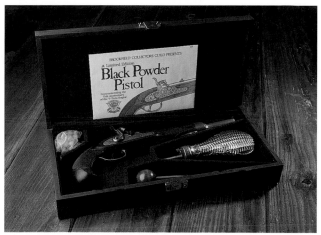

Black powder pistol, 1984

Above: In 1984, the Brookfield Collectors Guild offered this black powder pistol set to commemorate the seventy fifth anniversary of Harley-Davidson's V-twin engine. *Threedouble collection.*

1984 FXSB Low Rider

Left: Blame it on *Easy Rider*. Choppers had certainly been around before Captain America hit the road in the film, but after that movie they were big time. Everyone who wanted the *Easy Rider* look simply chopped everything extra off their bike that wasn't needed for motoring down the open road, hence the origin of the name. The Motor Company was sage in all of this, creating its factory chopper with the Super Glide series designed by Willie G. Davidson, grandson of one of the company founders. This 1984 FXSB featured the last year of the venerable Shovelhead engine before the debut of the Evolution. Owner: Ron Blackford.

Lighters and matches

Above: Back in the days when smoking cigarettes was actually thought to be good for one's health it was only natural for Harley-Davidson to promote its motorcycles on smoking paraphernalia. *Dudley Perkins Harley-Davidson collection.*

Lighter, 1960s

Left: A 1960s Harley-Davidson cigarette lighter. *Mike Parti collection.*

Knives

Facing page: Harley-Davidson has long issued commemorative knives. The top photo shows the 1978 (bottom) and 1991 knives. The bottom photo shows the eighty-fifth anniversary (top) and ninetieth anniversary knives, both of which were numbered, limited-edition specials. *Threedouble collection.*

Dealer matchbooks
Left: A selection of matchbooks issued by Harley-Davidson dealers across the United States. *Chris Haynes collection.*

Lighter, 1960s
Below, left: A 1960s Harley-Davidson cigarette lighter featuring an Electra-Glide etched into the metal body. *Dudley Perkins Harley-Davidson collection.*

Lighter, 1970s
Below, right: A 1970s cigarette lighter from the Dudley Perkins Company in San Francisco, California. *Dudley Perkins Harley-Davidson collection.*

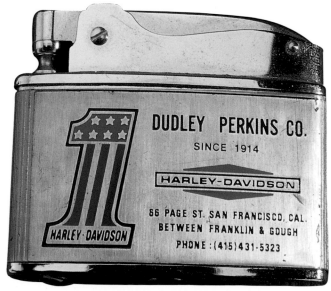

Lighter, 1993

Right: A Zippo cigarette lighter commemorating the ninetieth anniversary of the Motor Company in 1993. This lighter was produced in a numbered, limited edition of three thousand. *Dudley Perkins Harley-Davidson collection.*

Lighters

Below, left: A selection of Zippo cigarette lighters with various Harley-Davidson logos. *Chris Haynes collection.*

Lighters, 1960s

Below, right: Zippo cigarette lighters celebrating fifty years of Harley-Davidson racing. *Mike Parti collection.*

Ashtrays, 1962
While the Motor Company offered all sorts of smoking paraphernalia, these ashtrays would never have passed the official corporate censor. They were custom-made and ordered independently to promote the 1962 grand opening of Lake County Harley-Davidson Sales in the Painesville, Ohio, area. *Doug Leikala collection.*

Ashtrays, 1940s and 1950s

Left, top: A selection of metal Harley-Davidson dealer ashtrays from the 1940s and 1950s. *Doug Leikala collection.*

Ashtray

Left, center: A glass Harley-Davidson ashtray. *Paul Wheeler collection.*

Promotional items

Left, bottom: A selection of giveaway promotional items from the 1960s from Harley-Davidson of Long Beach, California, including jackknife and measuring tape key fobs, comb, and ashtray. *Threedouble collection.*

Cigarettes, 1990s

Below: Where there's smoke, there needs to be fire. Harley-Davidson long promoted its motorcycles with smoking paraphernalia so it was only natural that the company licensed Harley-Davidson brand cigarettes in the 1990s. *Mike Parti collection.*

Owners cards, 1960s

Above: Once you had become the proud owner of a new Harley-Davidson motorcycle in the 1960s, the company issued you an official owners card noting your name and motor serial number. The card fit snugly in your wallet alongside pictures of your family, your dog—and your new cycle. *Doug Leikala collection.*

Another happy owner, 1927

Right: With shaking hands ablur, another happy owner takes possession of his new Harley-Davidson from his friendly dealer. This wasn't just any motorcycling enthusiast, however: The new owner here is none other than aviator "Speed" Holman, winner of the 1927 National Air Races for piloting his aircraft from Cleveland, Ohio, to Spokane, Washington. Speed is shaking hands with Minneapolis, Minnesota, dealer George Faulders after taking delivery of his new Model 28. *Minnesota Historical Society collection.*

Chapter 2

On *the* Road

Touring Memorabilia, Club Pins, & Rider's Togs

In a 1970s ad slogan, the Motor Company articulated perfectly the alchemy that a Harley-Davidson motorcycle and the open road produce. The slogan read "The Great American Freedom Machine," and rarely has a copywriter gotten it so right.

The image of The Great American Freedom Machine was perfect for the 1970s, but it is also ideal for defining what a Harley-Davidson means for riders of almost any time and any place. Harley-Davidson motorcycles, whether vintage or new, are built for the road. In the pioneering days of the internal-combustion engine, a motorcycle signified speed, and speed signified freedom. Today, with the vista of a long stretch of blue highway unrolling before you, freedom—overused and hackneyed as the phrase may be—still best describes the sensation. And whether you are aiming your Harley-Davidson toward Sturgis, South Dakota, or any other point of the compass from Europe to Japan, Harley-Davidson is an American icon. The Milwaukee motorcycles are as indelibly linked to American pop culture as Coca-Cola, blue jeans, electric guitars, and Mickey Mouse.

The Motor Company has long been wise to all of this. And understanding that every owner wants to personalize his or her machine, Harley-Davidson has issued its accessory catalogs through the years, offering riders clothing and equipment for the road. These catalogs have carried everything from dice shifter knobs to leather jackets, windshields for your cycle to goggles for your eyes. All extend the Harley-Davidson mystique.

Touring memorabilia
 Harley-Davidson motorcycles were built for the road, and the Motor Company always provided plenty of touring accessories for their mechanical wares. For identification of the pictured items, see page 53. *Doug Leikala collection.*

Even more than the general motorcycle sales catalogs, the accessory catalog offers a vision of an era. The style of Harley-Davidson motorcycles has changed little over the years—best to call it a mechanical evolution. But the styles of clothing and other items in the accessory catalogs have changed dramatically over time, keeping pace with the fashions, fads, and fancies of the days. The 1928 accessory catalog, for example, offered "Inspected & Approved" Harley-Davidson items in a matter-of-fact graphic style similar to the famous Sears, Roebuck & Company mail-order catalogs of the time. By contrast, today's Harley-Davidson MotorClothes and collectibles catalog is a work of art with stylish design, stunning photographs, and a vast range of products.

Consider, for instance, the changes over the century in the fashions of riding wear—what were in the 1920s called "togs" and are today trademarked by Harley-Davidson as MotorClothes. In the 1928 accessory catalog, leather gaiters were almost a requirement for the avid motorcyclist. The engines of the day were fitted with the latest in total-loss oiling systems, meaning that as the oil was used, it was not recirculated, and the excess oil—hot, slippery, and messy as oil is—was spit out. Unless the rider were especially adroit at gymnastics, this spent oil typically landed on his or her knickers, making leather puttees a wise purchase. As one 1920s magazine ad noted with classic understatement, "You'll like them."

In 1941, the accessory catalog carried fabric or leather "English Military" riding breeches with wide, jodhpur-fashioned thighs and in a variety of colors to match motorcycle club uniforms. The "Slendo" model jodhpurs were available for women, because, as the catalog noted, "With motorcycling fast becoming one of the nation's foremost outdoor pastimes, it is inevitable that the fair sex should be taking a more active part in these activities. In doing so, they too, want to look their best garbed in neat, attractive, yet serviceable and practical riding togs."

In the 1990s, Harley-Davidson has its own licensed brand of blue jeans, tying one American icon with another. In addition, the 1990s MotorClothes line offers 1940s-style jodhpurs to riders seeking a retro look. The style has come full circle.

Today as in the early days, the most valuable item for riders in the accessory catalogs is no doubt the leather jacket. Don't underestimate it: A leather jacket is as important to a motorcyclist as gasoline in the tank and air in the tires. Leather jackets cut the wind, keep you warm, repel motor oil, and serve as a second skin in case of a fall. Accessory catalogs of the 1920s displayed a knee-length, double-breasted and belted leather coat that was proper yet dapper. By 1941, the catalog's horsehide leather jacket was cut "aviator style," no doubt influenced by the public's love of anything related to aviation in those days. By the 1990s, the MotorClothes line boasted more than thirty styles of leather jackets, from 1920s vintage cool to fringed suede coats for women and, to start them early, leather bomber jackets for six-year-olds.

Black leather jackets have long carried an aura of rebelliousness—as well as high style. They earned their outlaw mystique on the Fourth of July, 1947, in the sleepy hamlet of Hollister, California, when the Boozefighters Motorcycle Club descended on the town for a weekend of racing and revelry. Clowning for news photographer Barney Petersen, one motorcyclist clambered atop his Harley-Davidson Big Twin with a beer bottle in his hand and a staged—but probably well-practiced—drunken leer on his face while his buddies piled empties around the cycle. Petersen snapped the shutter, and *Life* magazine ran the posed photo with an outraged report that described the tomfoolery as a riot. The Hollister brouhaha inspired Stanley Kramer's 1953 film *The Wild One* with Marlon Brando as the rebel Johnny who wore his black leather jacket like a suit of armor. Following the Hollister rally and *The Wild One*'s debut, there was a time when a motorcycle rider who wished to be served at a roadside diner or not get thrown out of the local watering hole would shy away from wearing a black leather jacket. Today, all of that is but history, and many people wearing leather motorcycle jackets do not know which end of the motorcycle comes first.

Through the years, motorcycling has changed for better or worse; motorcycles have gone modern and then gone vintage; roads have been paved, widened, and stretched out to ever-farther horizons. But one thing has stayed the same: As past Motor Company President William H. Davidson once noted, "Styles may have changed, but motorcycle clothing either keeps you warm or it doesn't."

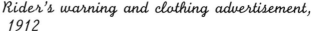

Rider's warning and clothing advertisement, 1912

As this tyrannical-looking salesman expounded, "Some riders use all their efforts and best judgment in selecting their motorcycle and then stop!!! Little do they think that half the pleasure of touring is the comfort of being properly equipped. To-day 'Gentlemen' are riding and unless you want to be classed otherwise consider your appearance." This ad from Nathan Novelty Mfg. Co. of New York City hawked motorcycle clothing and "leggins" at "prices to fit every purse." *Michael Dregni collection.*

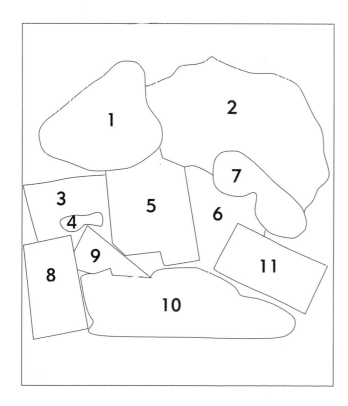

Touring memorabilia identification

Identification of the touring collectibles on page 50: 1. Brimmed rider's cap, 1950s; 2. Motorcycle club shirt belonging to "Dutchie" with Harley-Davidson and AMA patches, 1950s; 3. Harley-Davidson Mileage Club membership form, 1950s; 4. 25,000- and 50,000-mile (40,000- and 80,000-km) club lapel pins, 1950s; 5. Rally ribbons, 1950s; 6. Scarf, 1960s; 7. Goggles, 1930s; 8. Mileage notebook, 1920s; 9. Gypsy Tour pennant, 1950s; 10. Touring pins, patches, and belt buckles from the 1940s through the 1960s; 11. Postcard showing motorcycle touring club, 1910s.

Club jacket, 1950s
With these swank jackets embroidered with the American Motorcycle Association (AMA) emblem, there was no mistaking Hollywood Motorcycle Club members for the unsavory characters depicted in *The Wild One*. *Paul Wheeler collection.*

Jacket, 1950s
The Motor Company offered this classic 1950s-style summer jacket with a playful motorcycling image. *Doug Leikala collection.*

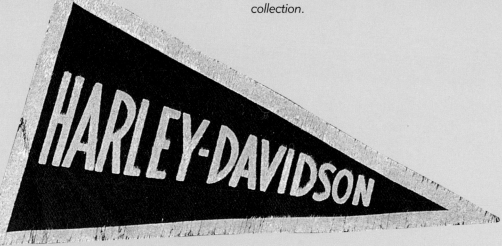

Pennants, 1950s
A Harley-Davidson pennant was just the thing for your cycle or to mark a place for your gang at a meet. As a 1950s accessory catalog boasted, "Ideal for clubs or vacation tours." *Doug Leikala collection.*

Key fobs

Once you owned your new Harley-Davidson, the first thing a dealer likely gave you was a fob to hold the key—and to remember the dealer. This is a small selection of fobs issued by just one dealer from the 1950s through the 1990s. *Dudley Perkins Harley-Davidson collection.*

1957 XL Sportster

The British were invading in full force in the 1950s: Nortons, Triumphs, and BSAs were threatening Harley-Davidson's and Indian's dominance on the racetracks and in the showrooms. Something needed to be done. Indian went the wrong route: It created a vertical twin and drove itself out of business. The Motor Company took the right route: It built a lightweight, 45-cubic-inch (750-cc) sports model, known as the K. It took a while to catch on, but the K gave way to the XL in 1957, and the Sportster line was born. Today, the Sportster is still going strong, and the British invasion is history. Owner: Mike Quinn.

"Cyclette" cap, 1950s

"Cyclettes" were motorcycle riders of the female persuasion in Harley-Davidson's lingo of the 1950s, and this specially designed brimmed cap was just the thing for the woman rider or pillion mate. As a 1950s accessory catalog boasted, "No need to bother with separate scarf and cap," as this chapeau was fitted with a scarf that could be tied under the chin to protect your bob from the wind. And always thinking of the latest fashions, the catalog noted that the Cyclette cap came in "Colors to match the boy friend's cap." *Threedouble collection*

Kidney belts, 1940s and 1950s

Kidney belts were as much a part of a Harley-Davidson rider's wardrobe in the 1940s and 1950s as a tattoo is today. As the 1941 accessory catalog explained to the uninitiated, "Many motorcyclists consider riding belts very necessary items of riding equipment for the body support and added comfort they impart, especially on long, extended trips." There were two reasons for the kidney belt's great popularity: Roads of the day were often not paved and thus needed regular grading and grooming to provide a comfortable ride. Secondly, Harley-Davidson motorcycles of the time did not have rear shock absorbers—and few riders wanted them! Comfort on a Harley-Davidson came from the motorcycle's seat, the rider's gluteus maximus, and the firm support of a kidney belt. *Threedouble collection.*

Dimmer Goggles, 1910s
Above: With the new craze for motorcycling, aftermarket firms popped up like mushrooms after a rain. Companies around the world offered everything for the cyclists, including Dimmer Goggles from the Chicago Eye Shield Company "for Day or Night riding" with special tinted lenses available in a variety of colors.

Goggles, 1930s–1940s
Right: In the days when the phrase "Eat my dust!" had real meaning due to the widespread lack of paved roads, a rider without goggles was looking for trouble. In its 1941 accessory catalog, Harley-Davidson termed its goggles "Eye Insurance" and offered six different models with several variations of each available, including aluminum frames, lamb binding, and more. Prices ranged from 95¢ for the plain-glass-lens Autocrat model to the $4.00 Greatview goggles for the well-heeled cyclist willing to splurge. *Paul Wheeler collection.*

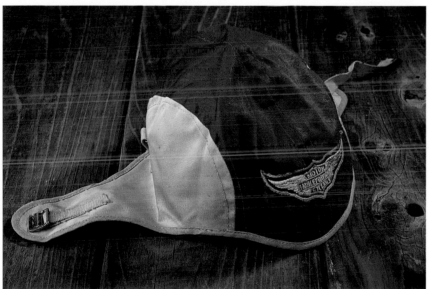

Cloth rider's cap, 1930s

Ever the style setter, Harley-Davidson offered its summer-weight cloth rider's cap in numerous one- and two-tone color schemes so the helmet would complement the look of your motorcycle club's riding jersey. These caps were available with or without the Harley-Davidson wing emblem. *Doug Leikala collection.*

Rider's brimmed caps, 1940s and 1950s

Above: Military-style brimmed rider's caps were high style for motorcyclists in the 1940s and 1950s with a look that said "classy," according to Harley-Davidson's 1941 accessory catalog. These caps were available in impressive-sounding "twillardine" cloth as well as brown leather and came with or without the Motor Company's wing emblem. The brims on all hats were made of black or white patent leather. The cloth hats were available in just about any color under the sun by special order so they were never out of step with your motorcycle club's color scheme and particular sense of style. *Doug Leikala collection.*

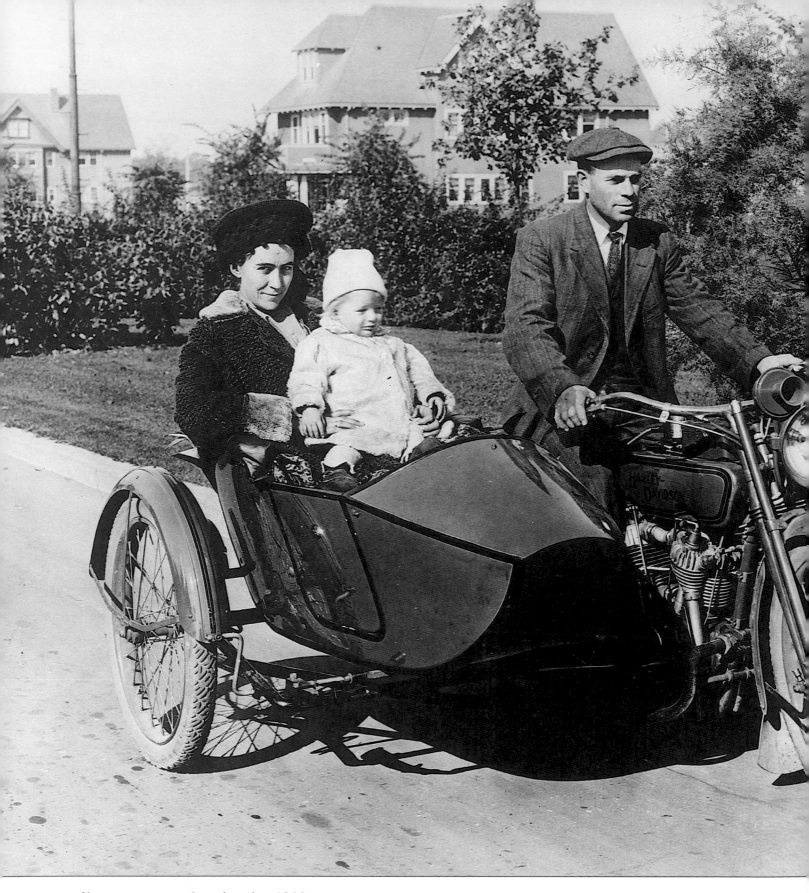

Happy motorcycling family, 1910s
The family that motorcycles together, stays together. Proud owner E. S. Moody of Minnesota takes the Moody clan for a spin in his V-twin sidecar rig. The coquettish Mrs. Moody obviously seems to be enjoying the outing—and the chance to wear her favorite motorcycling chapeau, to the envy of her friends no doubt. *Minnesota Historical Society collection.*

Aulogo motor cap, 1910s

Just as the motorcycle was a new invention, new fashions were in order for riders. The Aulogo hat was certainly "three caps in one." It not only protected your head from the elements but covered your mouth to shield your lungs from that noxious exhaust. The clear amber lens allowed you to view the passing scenery.

"Kant Leak" motorcycle suits, 1910s

Just the thing for a rainy ride, the Richard F. Hill Manufacturing Company of Newark, New Jersey, offered these stylish riding duds that "kant leak." Men's suits and women's skirts were offered for the well-dressed motorcycling duo.

Leather rider's cap, 1930s

Right, top: In the days before helmet laws, helmets were more of a fashion statement than a true lid protector, taking a styling cue from the aviators who were the cultural heroes of the era. Nevertheless, a 1940s accessory catalog stated, "Motorcyclists Prefer Helmets": This soft-leather rider's cap was the helmet Harley-Davidson had in mind. Numerous versions were offered, from gabardine cloth helmets for summer riding to sheep's wool-lined "glove leather" helmets for riding during "blustery weather" in the winter. *Paul Wheeler collection.*

Snap-brim caps, 1960s

Right, bottom: With a look that harkened back to the dawn of motorcycling, Harley-Davidson offered these vintage-style snap-brim caps to riders of the 1960s. *Doug Leikala collection.*

Brimmed hat, 1980s

Below: With helmet laws now in force in many places around the world, the dapper styling of yesteryear's rider's caps are all but forgotten. Still, Harley-Davidson dealers and independent vendors hawk licensed caps that serve a new purpose, unimaginable in the 1910s: These caps are essential for hiding the dreaded "helmet hair" look. *Chris Haynes collection.*

Leather gaiters, 1920s

In the early days of motorcycling, the most valuable item in the accessory catalog was probably a pair of these leather leggings. Harley-Davidson engines of the time consumed oil and spat it out after it was used in what was called total-loss oiling. This used oil invariably landed on the legs of the rider—and the oil was as hot, slippery, and dirty as oil can get. To protect your knickers or leather riding jodhpurs, these puttees were an essential part of every cyclist's wardrobe. Indian did away with total-loss oiling in 1933, but it was not until the debut of Harley-Davidson's savior, the 61-cubic-inch (1,000-cc) overhead-valve E Series Knucklehead of 1936, that the Motor Company inaugurated a dry oil sump and retired the total-loss system. With the coming of the 61 OHV, the Harley-Davidson faithful could finally hang up their leather gaiters. *Paul Wheeler collection.*

Gloves, 1961

It was the brave rider who dared to wear white leather gloves. *Threedouble collection.*

Dealer clothing sign, 1970s

Above: The Great American Freedom Machine inspired fashions that bridged the gap between 1970s chic and motorcycle utility. This dealer sign announced the new fashion statement. *Vince Spadaro collection.*

1977 XLCR

Right: In the days when café racers were the hot ticket and trick Ducati V-twins and Dunstall Nortons ruled the roost, Harley-Davidson designer Willie G. Davidson crafted a café racer of his own. Based on the Sportster, the XLCR blended styling lines from café racers, road racers, and dirt trackers, and wrapped the whole package in black with chromed highlights. But the XLCR was too much too soon and never sold well when new. Today, however, the world is a different place as witnessed by the latest Buell, and the XLCR is a hot commodity. Owner: Gary Aguirre.

Sweater, 1920s

"Some Class! That's what everybody will say when you step out in this Harley-Davidson racing jersey." Thus was the promise of a 1920s accessory catalog, offering rider's sweaters in a variety of "knock out" colors for "discriminating motorcycle riders." Special-order colors were also available for motorcycle clubs. The wing emblem was sewn to the sweater's chest. In addition, racing sweaters were available with the words "Harley-Davidson" in large felt letters. *Doug Leikala collection.*

1941 FL

Harley-Davidson's 61 OHV was first sold as a 1936 model with its 61-cubic-inch (1,000 cc) overhead-valve engine marking a new era in Motor Company history. In 1941, a 74-cubic-inch (1,200-cc) F Series version made its debut. This FL featured the high-compression engine. Owner: Armando Magri.

Club sweater, 1940s

The North Los Angeles Motorcycle Club rode in style with its members wearing white sweaters emblazoned with the club's logo. This club consisted of Bud Ekins, Jack Haley, Harry Pelton, and Homer Knapp; Knapp also raced a JD. Harley-Davidson sold these summer-weight sweaters to club members for $3.25 in the 1940s. *Mike Parti collection.*

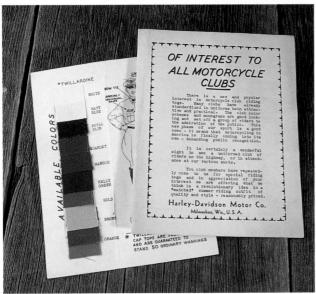

Sweater swatches, 1930s
Above, top: The Motor Company always catered to motorcycle clubs, as with this swatch card offering four sweater colors and "special trim" options. In all, Harley-Davidson promised clubs a total of 128 color combinations. *Doug Leikala collection.*

Club uniform swatches, 1930s
Above, bottom: "It is certainly a wonderful sight to see a uniformed club of riders on the highway, or in attendance at our various meets," this brochure noted. The Motor Company offered special-order uniforms to motorcycle clubs, warning clubs that had yet to order that "Many clubs have already standardized in uniforms both attractive and practical." *Doug Leikala collection.*

Endurance run riders, 1934
Above: "Iron butt" endurance rides separated the men from the boys and the women from the girls. This team entry in the 400-mile (640-km) Gopher Derby championship across Minnesota rode a mixture of Indians and a Harley-Davidson to first place. *Minnesota Historical Society collection.*

Windsock, 1936

Left: This miniature windsock came with a metal stand and rubber suction cup, and the accessory catalog advised you to mount it to your cycle's headlamp: "It makes neat advertising." *Doug Leikala collection.*

Race paddock, 1950s

Harley-Davidsons were built to be ridden—and some racers even rode their cycles to the racetrack, unbolted the lights and bolted on numberplates, and then rode for the checkered flag. This rider was preparing his bike for a race at the Minnesota State Fairgrounds. *Minnesota State Fair collection.*

Belt buckle, 1950s

Above: To hold up your new riding togs there was nothing like a belt secured with a buckle featuring a 1950s Hydra-Glide. Belt buckles have long been one of the most popular adornments in the pantheon of Harley collectibles. *Paul Wheeler collection.*

Belt buckle, 1958

Left: This brass belt buckle was awarded to a rider on the 1958 AMA tour. *Paul Wheeler collection.*

Jersey, 1950s

This spiffy two-tone black-and-orange jersey with the company's wing emblem was just the thing for the well-dressed cyclist in the 1950s. At the time, black leather motorcycle jackets stood for trouble in some people's eyes, as symbolized by Marlon Brando as Johnny in *The Wild One*. Following the July 4, 1947, brouhaha at Hollister, California, that was hyped by *Life* magazine and inspired Brando's movie, the black leather motorcycle jacket became a potent image for all that was wrong in the world. This jersey would have assured citizens that the wearer was not part of the bad element. *Doug Leikala collection.*

Ladies handbags, 1950s

For the woman rider who wanted to carry the Harley-Davidson style everywhere, these handbags matched the look of the Motor Company's leather saddle bags. Talk about a fashion statement! *Doug Leikala collection.*

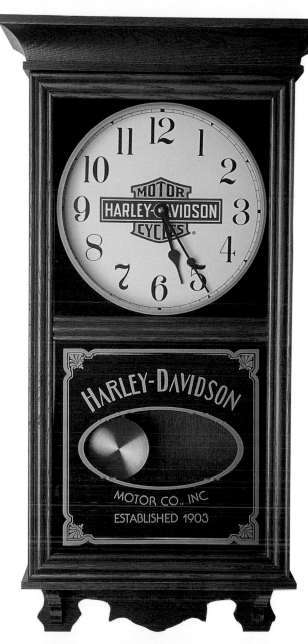

Wall clock, 1986
Left: Harley-Davidson's antique-replica wall clock commemorates the firm's founding in 1903. *Threedouble collection.*

Pocket watch, 1920s
Below, left: Harley-Davidson has long offered pocket watches to dealers and owners. This 1920s watch features the Motor Company's shield emblem. *Threedouble collection.*

Pocket watch, 1920s
Below, center: An elegant Harley-Davidson pocket watch from the 1920s. *Threedouble collection.*

Pocket watch, 1920s
Below, right: A simple, Elgin-made Harley-Davidson pocket watch from the 1920s. *Threedouble collection.*

Watch fobs

Above: Miscellaneous fobs from the Motor Company's history. From left, 1950s fob, 1920s shield, and 1910s postal promotional medal. *Doug Leikala collection.*

Watch fobs, 1910s

Right: Since a pocket watch was the rage in motorcycling's early years, watch fobs that attached to the watch's handle were a common item given away by dealers as promotion or by motorcycling groups as mementos. From left, these fobs were awarded to riders at the 1912 FAM tour, the 1914 FAM tour, and the 1918 National Motorcycle Gypsy Tour. *Mike Parti collection.*

Watches, 1990s
Above: A complete set of Harley-Davidson's collector series of watches that were packaged in replica oil cans. *Threedouble collection.*

Pocket watch, 1993
Left: The Motor Company offered this limited-edition ninetieth anniversary watch in 1993 to commemorate the Reunion in Milwaukee, the ride of hundreds of Harley-Davidson riders nationwide to the factory. *Threedouble collection.*

1914 V-twin

The glory days of the Silent Gray Fellow singles were numbered when Harley-Davidson unveiled its first V-twin in 1909. Sure, the twins took time to catch on, and the Motor Company continued to produce singles until 1934, but that first V-twin showed the shape of things to come. This 1914 single-speed V-twin originates from only the fifth year of V-twin production, as no V-twins were offered in 1910. Owner: Ray Ebersole.

Tie clasps, 1910s and 1920s

To keep your Harley-Davidson four-in-hand tie in place while motoring, a Motor Company tie clasp was just the thing. The accessory catalog offered a variety of patterned and colorful ties made of leather designed to simulate silk, as the catalog copy broadcasted, "Look Like Silk, Wear Like Iron." The ties were marketed to police officers, firefighters, postal carriers, and anyone else who wanted to look dapper while cycling. *Doug Leikala collection.*

Medals, 1900s and 1910s

The Federation of American Motorcyclists was founded in 1901, but was always strapped for cash and worried by allegations of unfair racing rules; after two decades of rocky history, it gave way to the American Motorcycle Association (AMA) in 1924. These FAM endurance run medals date from a 1905 Waltham, Massachusetts, meet, similar to the run won by Walter Davidson in 1908, and a 1914 meet. *Doug Leikala collection.*

Meet pins, 1910s

The Gypsy Tour pin from June 16–17, 1917, commemorates a run. The October 4, 1919, mechanic's pass is from a national championship race. *Doug Leikala collection.*

Club badge

Left: This badge from the Motor Cycling Club notes that the club was founded in 1901, at the dawn of motorcycling's history. *Doug Leikala collection.*

Motorcycle club meet, 1919

The Minneapolis Motor Cycle Club saddles up for an outing. Belonging to a motorcycling club was de rigueur in the early days of cycling. Camaraderie, picnics, and sharing tips for maintaining the early mounts was all part of the fun. The cyclists here are bundled up for warmth on this autumn day with riding gear including anything and everything from bowler derbies to woolen double-breasted dress coats—and one women sidecar passenger even donned a fur pillbox hat (second cycle from right). *Minnesota Historical Society collection.*

Lapel pins

Enamel-painted metal lapel pins are a favored memento of runs, meets, and races. This is a small selection of pins from around the world, dating from the 1950s through the 1990s. *Dudley Perkins Harley-Davidson collection.*

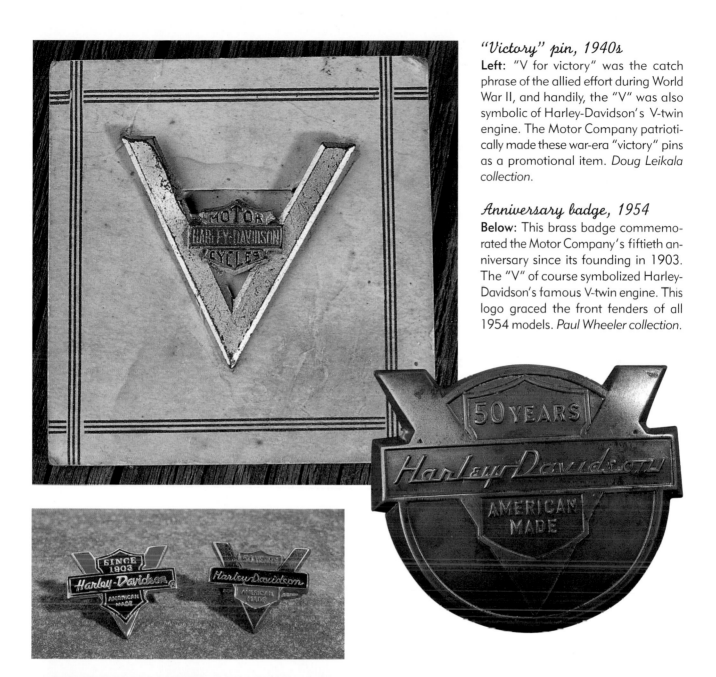

"Victory" pin, 1940s

Left: "V for victory" was the catch phrase of the allied effort during World War II, and handily, the "V" was also symbolic of Harley-Davidson's V-twin engine. The Motor Company patriotically made these war-era "victory" pins as a promotional item. *Doug Leikala collection.*

Anniversary badge, 1954

Below: This brass badge commemorated the Motor Company's fiftieth anniversary since its founding in 1903. The "V" of course symbolized Harley-Davidson's famous V-twin engine. This logo graced the front fenders of all 1954 models. *Paul Wheeler collection.*

Lapel pins, 1954 and 1990s

Left, top: The lapel pin on the right commemorated Harley-Davidson's fiftieth anniversary in 1954, while the pin on the left retained the early style into the 1990s. *Dudley Perkins Harley-Davidson collection.*

Lapel pins, 1930s and 1960s

Left: The wing emblem has lasted throughout the Motor Company's long history. These Harley-Davidson lapel pins date from the 1930s (top) and 1960s. *Doug Leikala collection.*

The Harley-Davidson Enthusiast, 1916

Harley-Davidson launched its owner magazine, *The Harley-Davidson Enthusiast*, in 1916, to broadcast the Motor Company's latest and greatest exploits and inspire loyalty to the brand. Harley-Davidson initially termed the magazine a "now-and-then" publication, meaning that it was published every now and then. This August 1916 issue would be followed by many more issues through the years. The Motor Company was inconsistent in how it titled the magazine: In the beginning and through the 1920s, it was *The Harley-Davidson Enthusiast*, but the exact wording of the title changed numerous times in the following decades and the magazine appeared under the name *Harley-Davidson Enthusiast* in the 1930s, *The Enthusiast* in the 1950s and at other times, and *The Motorcycle Enthusiast in Action* in the 1950s and 1960s, although the magazine is commonly referred to as *The Enthusiast*. Still published today, *The Enthusiast* is the world's longest-running motorcycle magazine. *Mike Parti collection.*

The Harley-Davidson Enthusiast, 1920s

Harley-Davidson often featured police motorcyclists on the cover of the owner magazine as police fleet sales were big business for the Motor Company. *Chris Haynes collection.*

The Enthusiast, 1940s

Along with inspiring loyalty to Harley-Davidson, *The Enthusiast* also spurred Indian to create its own magazine, *Indian News*. *Chris Haynes collection.*

Motorcycling books, 1910s

Many of the mechanical marvels of the 1910s and 1920s were of wonder to the era's children, and books featuring the newfangled machines made for great bedtime reading. Thus, there were series of popular novels about the Submarine Boys, Battleship Boys, Tom Swift and his fanciful creations, and much more. *Bert Wilson's Twin Cylinder Racer* by J. W. Duffield captured the excitement of boardtrack racing, the most dramatic and bloodthirsty of motorcycling sports. Ralph Marlow's The Big Five Motorcycle Boys series saw the gang travel to the Tennessee Wilds and further afield in some six titles. Other famous children's motorcycling books included *Tom Swift and His Motorcycle* by Victor Appleton, two long-running Motorcycle Chums series by Lieutenant Howard Payson and Andrew Carey Lincoln, and *The Motor Scout* by Herbert Strang. *Chris Haynes collection.*

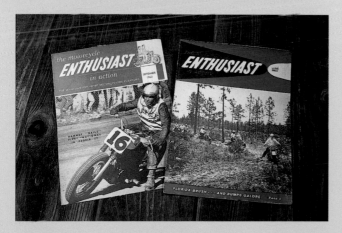

The Motorcycle Enthusiast in Action, 1960s

The 1960s saw yet another change in design style to keep the owner magazine up with the times. *Chris Haynes collection.*

The Enthusiast, 1950s

Two issues of *The Enthusiast* still in their original mailing envelopes. *Chris Haynes collection.*

Chapter 3

Racing
for the
Checkered Flag

Race Goods, Meet Posters, & Competition Memorabilia

When and where the first motorcycle race was held is long forgotten, but motorcycle racing was probably born on some fateful day in history when two motorcyclists on their mounts met on a road for the first time. They naturally had to see who had the faster cycle, Harley-Davidson or Indian.

The need for speed went hand in hand with the development of the motorcycle. Legend has it that the first motorcycle in North America was a steam-powered, wood-framed "velocipede" crafted by Sylvester H. Roper of Roxbury, Massachusetts, in the late 1860s. The story goes that Gottlieb Daimler, of the former German state of Württemberg, built the first gasoline-powered motorcycle, going for an inaugural ride on his creation on November 10, 1885. Roper and Daimler had one thing in common: They were both men of mechanical aptitude in a time when creating their own mechanicals was essential.

In North America, it was the meeting of the minds of George Hendee and Oscar Hedstrom that produced in 1901 the first commercially viable "motocycle"—as they termed it in those days before there was such a word for a motorized bicycle—and christened it the Indian. Hendee was an avid bicycle racer, and he commissioned Hedstrom to develop a motorized bicycle as a mechanized pacer for bicycle racing. Little did Hendee or Hedstrom realize what their creation would become.

Racing memorabilia
The Motor Company first went racing in 1914, and following big wins at the 1915 300-mile (480-km) road races in Venice, California, and Dodge City, Kansas, Harley-Davidson had racing in its blood. For identification of the pictured items, see page 86. *Doug Leikala collection.*

William S. Harley and his next-door neighbor and boyhood friend, Arthur Davidson, shared a similar passion for "motocycles." The story of the 1903 creation of the first Harley-Davidson motorcycle in a 10x15-foot (250x375-cm) shed behind the Davidson family's Milwaukee home has become legend, akin to that of the birth of a certain baby in a manger some 2,000 years ago. William S. Harley and Arthur Davidson were both in their twenties, and together with Davidson's brothers, Walter and William A., and father, William C., they all learned as they created.

The first Harley-Davidsons were not created for speed, however. Harley and the Davidsons sought to build reliable, viable motorized transportation, and the fledgling Motor Company did not officially enter motorcycle racing during the first decade of its existence. In the early days, Harley-Davidson had strict house rules forbidding race support.

It was not until 1914, after eleven years of developing, producing, and selling motorcycles as transportation, that Harley-Davidson turned to racing. That change in corporate policy was to forever change Harley-Davidson—and the motorcycle world. Following its first important victories—at the 1915 300-mile (480-km) road races in Venice, California, and Dodge City, Kansas—the Motor Company had racing in its blood.

For the next four decades, Harley-Davidson and Indian waged war on the racetracks of the United States—and the world. The war was for the checkered flag, the trophy, and the trophy girl's kiss just as much as it was for sales of motorcycles on the showroom floor. Racing improved the breed and proved the breed, and a win on Sunday meant sales on Monday, as the racing team managers always pitched the Motor Company executives.

Through the years, Harley-Davidson has won its fair share of races, from the pine-board motordromes of the 1910s to Daytona Superspeedway's banked tri-oval. The Motor Company has created many memorable racing motorcycles, including its great "Peashooter" singles of the 1920s, the iron-willed KR, the all-conquering and long-lived XR-750, and the late, great VR-1000. And over time, racing at Harley-Davidson has grown from a sport to become a business, and then grown from a business to become a passion.

Racing memorabilia
Identification of the competition collectibles sampling on page 84: 1. Postcard showing the Columbus (Ohio) Motordrome, 1910s; 2. Raffle ticket and hill climb advertisement, 1930s; 3. Hubley cast-iron motorcycle racer, 1930s; 4. Pit pass, 1930s; 5. Dodge City, Kansas, patch, 1953; 6. Daytona Beach, Florida, postcard, 1950s; 7. Harley-Davidson race wins card, 1948; 8. Watkins Glen, New York, race official arm band, 1958; 9. Race official name pin, 1962; 10. Hill climb ticket, 1933; 11. Racer Russell Smiley fan postcard, 1910s; 12. Race pins and watch fobs from the 1920s through the 1950s; 13. Hill climb motorcycle hang ticket, 1927; 14. Driver pass to hang on shirt button, 1930s; 15. Hill climb ticket stub, 1920s.

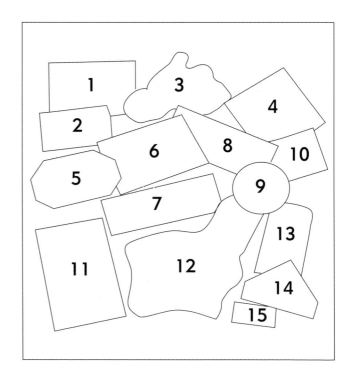

Starting line, 1913

An array of Indians, Excelsiors, and Harley-Davidsons await the wave of the flag to start a dirt-track race around the Minnesota State Fairgrounds. The Motor Company may not have officially entered motorcycle races before 1913, but that didn't stop many a Harley-Davidson owner from rolling his or her pride and joy up to the starting line and defending Milwaukee's honor. *Minnesota State Fair collection.*

Red Parkhurst photographs, 1920s

Left: Leslie "Red" Parkhurst (number 7) was one of Harley-Davidson's secret weapons. In the photo at top, he is pictured astride an eight-valve racer; in the bottom photo, he is putting on his gloves to pilot a sidecar rig. *Mike Parti collection.*

Motordrome program, 1913

Motordrome boardtrack racing was at its peak around 1910 before the move was made to long boardtracks in the mid-1910s. Harley-Davidson did not officially sanction racing during these early years, but riders like Red Parkhurst proved themselves on these "saucer tracks" before joining the Motor Company's race team. *Mike Parti collection.*

Boardtrack racing photographs, 1920s

Period photographs of 1920s boardtrack racing action. *Mike Parti collection.*

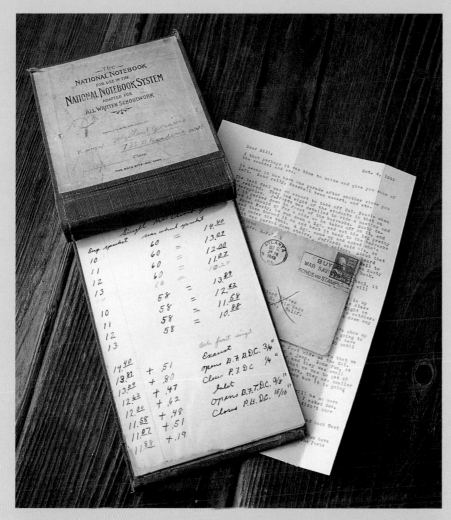

Hill climb notes, 1927–1930

Every racer has his or her secret black book of tuning notes: This school notebook belonged to Harley-Davidson hill climber Bill Graves. *Mike Parti collection.*

Racing carburetor, 1910s

Once Harley-Davidson committed itself to racing, it was in up to its neck. In the war with Indian and Excelsior, Harley-Davidson initially had to play catch-up to match the dominant firms' technical development. But the Motor Company was soon taking its share of checkered flags with new frames, Two Cam motors, and more for both the V-twins and the Peashooter singles. This "Big Air" racing carburetor for the eight-valve V-twins of the 1910s had a unique rotating intake collar that increased air intake. It was a secret weapon and trick racing part of its day. *Mike Parti collection.*

Racing memorabilia, 1940s

Right: An AMA membership card from 1947 and a selection of photographs of racer and AMA referee Jack Wilson of Chattanooga, Tennessee, from the good old days of racing. Wilson raced a Harley-Davidson WR for a time, but the photo at bottom shows him on a BSA. He also worked as a stunt man and was an early pioneer in roller derbies. *Mike Parti collection.*

Race trophy, 1930s

Left: The AMA was the prime sanctioning body for motorcycle racing in the United States by the 1930s. This trophy would have been a prized award—along with the trophy girl's kiss. *Doug Leikala collection.*

Daytona race programs, 1940s

Above: Daytona Beach, Florida, has long been a worldwide headquarters for speed. In the olden days before the Daytona Superspeedway was built, automobile pilots and motorcycle riders sought to set speed records on the long, flat—and beautiful—beaches. A race course was soon organized with roughly half the oval circuit run on a paved beach frontage road and the other half on the sand. This blend of surfaces made for tough racing, but the most difficult aspect was undoubtedly the corners. Thus, the 1947 Daytona race program (right) was not bragging too much when its termed the national championships as the "World's Greatest Motorcycle Races." The other program dates from 1941. *Threedouble collection.*

Race program and tickets, 1939

Left: Once Harley-Davidson entered racing in 1914, it did so with gusto. The 1920s and 1930s witnessed some of the fiercest battles between the racers of the Motor Company and Indian. These 1939 race programs and tickets for 100- and 200-mile (160- and 320-km) championship races in Chattanooga, Tennessee, would have been fought to the bitter end. *Threedouble collection.*

Racing jersey, 1940s
The Motor Company offered racing jerseys with its name sewn on in large black felt letters to privateers riding the firm's wares. The 1941 accessory catalog shows a rider wearing the sweater—with a dress shirt and tie underneath! The 1941 price was $6.25. *Threedouble collection.*

Matchbooks, 1930s
Matchbooks were ideal advertising "billboards" for race events in the early years of motorcycling, and these two announce hill climbs in Cary, Illinois (left), and Muskegon, Michigan. *Doug Leikala collection.*

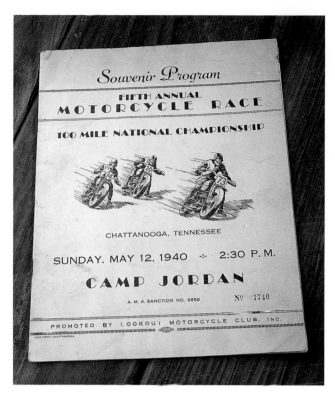

Race program, 1940
A 1940 race program for a 100-mile (160-km) national championship at Chattanooga, Tennessee. *Threedouble collection.*

Race programs, 1939
These 1939 race programs heralded TT races, which were derived—at least in name—from the legendary Tourist Trophy races on the Isle of Man, between Wales and England. Yet while the Manx races were held on roads, American TT races featured an odd mix of road and off-road riding, which in turn gave birth to a specialized style of riding and distinctive racing motorcycles built to handle both surfaces. *Threedouble collection.*

Racing fobs, 1930s
These fobs, given out by Harley-Davidson, promoted "The Motorcycle Magnificent" for its endurance, power, and speed. *Doug Leikala collection.*

Race poster, 1950s
Racing competition between archenemies Harley-Davidson and Indian reached a peak in the early 1950s, as promoted by this meet poster depicting a Milwaukee product on the left and presumably a racer from the Wigwam—an Indian rider—on the right. *Chris Haynes collection.*

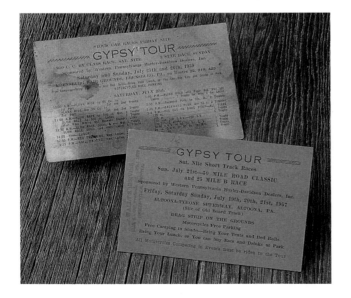

Race advertisements, 1950s
These handcards announced Gypsy Tour races for 1957 (right) at Altoona, Pennsylvania, "Site of Old Board Track," and 1959, both sponsored by Western Pennsylvanian Harley-Davidson Dealers, Inc. Among the events were short-track races, drag races, slow races, and blindfold races. As the 1957 advertisement notes, "All Motorcycles Competing in Events must be riden [sic] to the Tour." Those were the days. *Doug Leikala collection.*

Trophy winner, 1950s

Another black-and-orange rider takes home a trophy, this time at a dirt-track race at the Minnesota State Fairgrounds grandstand. The competition in the 1950s between Harley-Davidson and Indian racers was fierce and cutthroat, mirroring the competition for sales dollars on the dealers's showroom floors. *Minnesota State Fair collection.*

Race sculpture

Left: A race winner astride his WR holds a trophy aloft in this sculpture by artist Leigh Wulle. *Mike Parti collection.*

Iron cycle, iron man, 1950s

Left: Harley-Davidson star Brad Andres ready for action on his KR. Racing gear in the 1950s was minimalistic, at best. Andres here wears leather pants, a leather jacket with a racing vest over the top, and his smartest leather work boots. A helmet and goggles completed the picture. *Michael Dregni collection.*

Race trophy, 1946

Below: AMA trophy for the 1946 Cactus Derby with first place in the solo class going to D. M. Gantenbein, who amassed one thousand points. *Chris Haynes collection.*

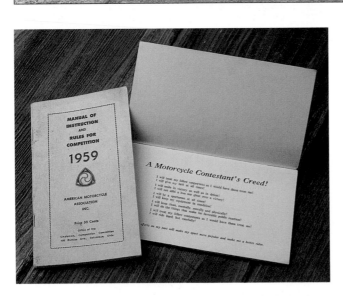

Rule books, 1959

The Golden Rule extended to motorcycle racing in the AMA's "A Motorcycle Contestant's Creed." As the last line of the creed promised, "I will ride hard, but carefully!" *Mike Parti collection.*

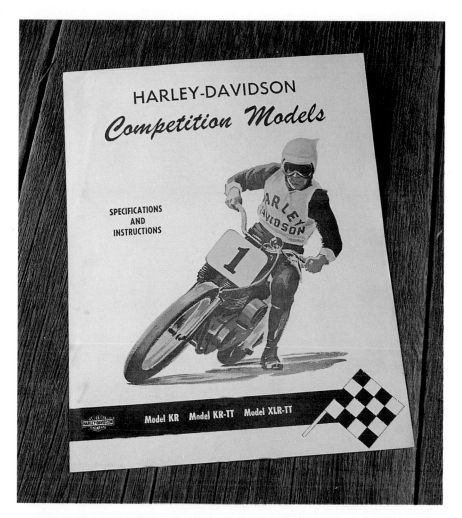

Racing literature, 1950s
Left: Harley-Davidson's KR carried the company's banner against Indian and the British invasion from its debut in 1952 to its demise in 1968 when the XR appeared on the scene. Even then, the Motor Company's factory riders sometimes parked their iron-head XRs in favor of the old tried-and-true KRs. This brochure gave specifications and instructions for the KR and its variants, the KR-TT and the Sportster-based XLR-TT. *Doug Leikala collection.*

Daytona race buttons, 1950s
Below: A collection of souvenir buttons from Daytona motorcycle races of the 1950s. *Doug Leikala collection.*

Harley-Davidson KR-TT

The ultimate in racing collectibles: Harley-Davidson's iron-willed road racer, the KR-TT, and a set of original Motor Company racing leathers. *Photo by Michael Dregni.*

Hat with finisher pins, 1960s and 1970s
This leather hat is covered with pins awarded to finishers of races and tours. *Mike Parti collection.*

Race program, 1967
After battling Indian for decades, Harley-Davidson had new contenders for the crown in the 1950s and 1960s: the British invasion, lead by Triumph, BSA, and Norton, with AJS/Matchless, Velocette, and Vincent nipping at their heels. The bold, straight-on graphics of this Reading, Pennsylvania, race program could only hint at the action that was to take place. *Threedouble collection.*

Racing literature, 1970s

Right: Harley-Davidson's iron XR-750 was to be the Motor Company's savior on the racing front in 1969 against the rising sun of Japanese motorcycles, but things did not quite work out that way. The iron XRs did not perform up to snuff, and many black-and-orange riders brought their KRs back out of retirement. With the reworked aluminum XR of 1972, however, Harley-Davidson served notice that it meant business, and the XR-750 went on to become one of the winningest motorcycles ever. *Doug Leikala collection.*

race-ready dirt track racer
ready to race for mile and half mile ovals
the newest Out-Performer

Dirt-tracking, 1980s

Right: Harley-Davidson hero Jay Springsteen tucks in on his Bill Werner–tuned XR-750. *Michael Dregni collection.*

Ascot winners buckle, 1968

Below: A brass belt buckle awarded to the 1968 Ascot (California) Speedway race winner. *Mike Parti collection.*

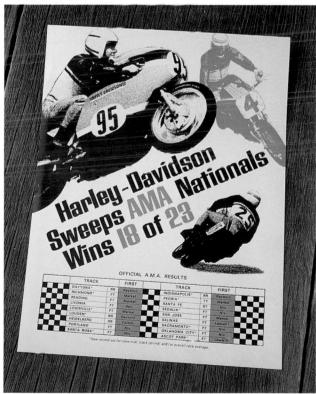

Racing literature, 1965

Above: To combat the lightweight British Triumphs and Italian Parillas and Ducatis on American turf, Harley-Davidson chose not to develop its own 250-cc motorcycle but went straight to the source. In 1960, Harley-Davidson bought a half stake in Aermacchi of Varese, Italy, and began importing the firm's Ala Verde 250-cc horizontal single, renaming it the Sprint for the North American market. The Motor Company also bought Aermacchi's racing expertise, which it first used dramatically at Daytona in 1963, when Dick Hammer and his factory Sprint (in Italy, the race version was called the Ala d'Oro, or "Gold Wing," back before Honda got hold of the name) beat Norris Rancourt on his Parilla. *Doug Leikala collection.*

Racing poster, 1968

Left: The year 1968 was the last hurrah for the old KR, Harley-Davidson's stalwart race winner. As this promotional poster shouted, the Motor Company won eighteen of twenty-three AMA nationals—although amazingly it lost the championship (which this poster fails to tell you) to Gary Nixon and his Triumph. Still, the KR had a last blaze of glory with Cal Rayborn winning Daytona after all the other KRs broke or crashed. *Doug Leikala collection.*

Chapter 4

Motorcycle Toys

Cast-Iron, Pressed-Metal, & Plastic Motorcycles in Miniature

When Mom or Dad went out to the garage to kick over their Big Twin, Junior and Sis naturally began wishing for a motorcycle of their own. The sound, the style, and simply the fact that their parents—or that black-sheep uncle or aunt—had a Harley-Davidson were all inspiration to impressionable young minds. While Junior and Sis had to wait until they grew up to throw their leg over a big, iron machine, they could at least have a miniature cast-iron or pressed-metal motorcycle to call their very own.

Astute toy makers began producing elfin version of the big bikes in the 1920s when the motorcycle first caught the public's attention and began to satisfy the human desire for speed. For a time at the dawn of the motorcycle's creation, daring young riders on their glorious, green Harley-Davidsons and stunning, red Indians were watched with awe by mere citizens who likened their exploits to those of famous and beloved aviators such as Charles Lindbergh. It was only natural that toy makers rushed to craft miniature motorcycles for youngsters to roar around their bedrooms.

Toy motorcycles fashioned from pressed steel were first made in the 1910s in Europe. The pressed steel was often covered with tin to inhibit rusting, and so these toys are sometimes termed "pressed-tin" miniatures. The metal was then either hand painted or, more often, printed with lithographic designs. German firms were prolific pressed-metal toy makers, including the world's senior toy maker, Gebrüder Märklin of Nuremberg, as well as Tipp & Company, Gebrüder Einfalt,

Motorcycle toys
Miniature motorcycles provided inspiration, education, and hours of fun to children—of all ages—around the world. For identification of the pictured items, see page 104. *Doug Leikala collection.*

Müller & Kadeder (M & K), Ernst Paul Lehmann, Arnold, Georg Levy, and others. French manufacturers Jouet and Luxia, English makers such as Mettoy and J. G. Brenner & Company (Brenco), Italian firms INGAP and S. Ferrari, and Spanish firms such as Rico and Paya Cooperative all crafted pressed-metal motorcycles. Starting in the 1930s, Japanese companies such as Masudaya, Marusan, Nomura, Hadson, and others made similar miniatures, sometimes bearing the Harley-Davidson name but rarely its licensing. In North America, the primary pressed-metal toy maker was the grand Louis Marx & Company of New York City, which crafted numerous styles of motorcycle toys from the 1920s until World War II.

These miniature, pressed-metal cycles often featured wind-up, spring-powered "motors"; battery-powered headlamps; and even wind-up sirens on the police models. The pressed-metal toys were printed with detailed images of the cycle's engine and other components, all of which was a good primer for a youngster's motorcycling education.

In addition to the high-quality pressed-metal toys, miniature motorcycles were fashioned of a variety of other materials throughout the world. Cast lead, rubber, sheet metal, and finally plastic were all used to make toys. In the 1950s, die-casting of metal, and, eventually, molding of plastics, were perfected as inexpensive techniques for high-volume production of toys.

Starting in the 1920s, American toy manufacturers cast molten gray iron—an inexpensive iron alloy with a high carbon content—in molds to create replicas of the Harley-Davidsons, Indians, Excelsiors, and

Hendersons of the day. The replicas were never exact, but they were as detailed as the medium of cast iron allowed, and discerning youngsters could often tell a Harley-Davidson from an Indian.

American cast-iron toy makers included Arcade Manufacturing Company of Freeport, Illinois; Champion Hardware Company of Geneva, Ohio; Kilgore Manufacturing Company of Westerville, Ohio; and others. But the majority of cast-iron motorcycles in North America were made by the famed Hubley Manufacturing Company of Lancaster, Pennsylvania, whose early motto for their toys was, "They're Different." The firm itself was also different: Hubley was farsighted in the ways of licensing and marketing, so farsighted that in the 1920s the company signed agreements with numerous major manufacturers of the era from Packard to Maytag, Indian to Harley-Davidson, giving Hubley exclusive rights to manufacture replica toys with a firm's logo. Thus, almost all toy motorcycles in North America bearing the Harley-Davidson name were cast-iron Hubley models.

Hubley continued to make cast-iron toys up until the early days of World War II, when material shortages curbed the firm's toy business. The company ceased cast-iron toy production in 1942, but many of Hubley's classic toys survive. Youth may be but a memory, but the motorcycling mementos of childhood roll on.

Toy motorcycles

Identification of the motorcycle toys on page 102: 1. Pressed-steel, battery-powered G-man motorcycle made by Hadson of Japan in the 1950s; 2. Cast-iron police sidecar rig made by Hubley in the 1920s and fitted with a loop on the front fender to which a pull string could be attached; 3. Cast-iron Popeye Patrol made by Hubley in 1938; 4. Cast-iron Hubley police cycle, 1930s; 5. Bent-metal stand-up military motorcycle figure; 6. Plastic die-cast sidecar rig; 7. Early plastic die-cast toy with metallic paint, 1940s; 8. Early plastic die-cast police rider made by Auburn Rubber of the United States, 1950s; 9. Early die-cast police toy, 1940s; 10. Cast-iron Hubley toy, 1930s; 11. Early plastic die-cast Servi-car toy made by Acme Toy Works of Chicago, 1940s.

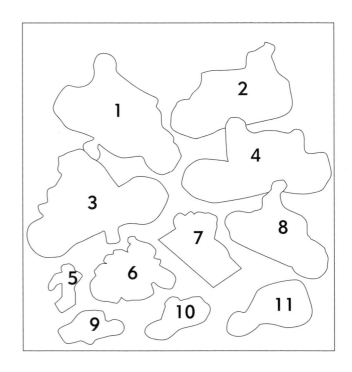

Toy motorcycles, 1930s
A trio of Hubley cast-iron Harley-Davidsons from the 1930s in a variety of colors, riding on stylish, white-rubber tires. Over the years, the Motor Company at times offered Hubley's licensed toys for sale through *The Enthusiast* magazine. *Doug Leikala collection.*

Toy motorcycle, 1930s

Above: A cast-iron Harley-Davidson V-twin with police rider from the 1930s made by Hubley. The prominent American toy maker was founded in 1894 by John E. Hubley, and over the years was prolific in producing hundreds of thousands of toys, from motorcycles to automobiles and cap guns to dollhouse stoves. Many a youth played with a Hubley toy at one time or another. *Doug Leikala collection.*

Toy motorcycle, 1930s

Right: A cast-iron Harley-Davidson–style motorcycle with sidecar from the 1930s, believed to have been made by the Champion Hardware Company. Champion was started in 1883 by John and Ezra Hasenpflug as an iron foundry that did contract castings for manufacturers of everything from window locks to building hardware. It was not until 1930 that the firm branched out to make cast-iron toys, a venture that lasted only until 1936. *Doug Leikala collection.*

Police patrol, 1940

Two of the Minneapolis, Minnesota, police force's finest sit astride their Harley-Davidsons, ready for action. The officer on the right is obviously pleased with his mount. The officer on the left may just be biding his time until he can twist that throttle open and hit the road. *Minnesota Historical Society collection.*

Toy motorcycle, 1930s
Left: A Hubley cast-iron Harley-Davidson with Parcel Post sidecar from the 1930s. *Doug Leikala collection.*

Toy motorcycles, 1930s

Above, top: A duo of cast-iron Harley-Davidson–style motorcycles from the 1930s, made either by Hubley or Kilgore. The toy in the back has a pillion rider. *Doug Leikala collection.*

Toy motorcycle, 1930s

Above, bottom: A piece of history: "Crash cars" were the forerunners of today's first-response emergency paramedic teams, sort of a combination fire engine and ambulance rolled into one. They rushed to the scene of automotive accidents to provide first aid to injured motorists and help with damaged vehicles. This Hubley cast-iron Harley-Davidson crash car dates from the 1930s. As with many of its cast-iron models, Hubley also made similar versions of this toy but with Indian "specifications." *Paul Wheeler collection.*

Police toys

Above: A selection of police toys from Hubley and other manufacturers spanning a broad spectrum of time. The grand police rider with sidecar (top right) was made of pressed steel by Marx in the 1940s and featured a spring-wound motor and siren. *Chris Haynes collections.*

Toy motorcycle, 1950s

Above: Following World War II, Hubley set aside its cast-iron toy manufacturing and switched to the modern die-casting techniques. This 1950s Harley-Davidson with removable police rider is an example of Hubley's die-cast toys. *Doug Leikala collection.*

Toy motorcycle, 1930s

Right: A Hubley cast-iron police Harley-Davidson from the 1930s. This toy featured a battery-powered headlamp; the toy was hinged, allowing you to place the battery inside. *Threedouble collection.*

Toy motorcycles

Above: A selection of toy motorcycles from numerous manufacturers and several eras. The VR-1000 (top left) with famous Harley-Davidson rider Miguel Duhamel's number was made by the Ertl Company of Dyersville, Iowa, and sold at dealerships to commemorate the Motor Company's return to road racing. The Mickey Mouse and Donald Duck cycles were made of pressed steel in the 1950s by the Lin Mar Company of Japan. The large police rider (bottom right) is a reproduction of an original Hubley cast-iron toy. *Chris Haynes collection.*

Toy motorcycles

Left, top: Plastic toys began to replace the old-fashioned metal toys in the 1950s. Louis Marx & Company, the famous manufacturer of glorious pressed-metal toys, was at the forefront of the new plastic casting. Marx unveiled its Fix-All line of plastic toys, which included these 1953 Harley-Davidsons, complete with rubber tires, battery-powered headlamp, kickstand, saddlebags, and a set of plastic tools. *Doug Leikala collection.*

Promotional toy motorcycle, 1958

Left, bottom: To promote its new Duo-Glide, with suspension now at both ends, the Motor Company issued this plastic promotional FLH in 1958. *Doug Leikala collection.*

Chapter 5

Servicing Harley-Davidson

Maintenance Materials, Fluids, Tools, Parts, & Paints

Harley-Davidson owners have Francisco "Pancho" Villa to thank for the quality of motorcycle maintenance information that has been passed down through the decades.

In 1916, the Mexican revolutionary hero was angered by American support of the power-hungry and corrupt Mexican government, so Villa retaliated by sending raiding parties across the U.S.–Mexican border into Texas. President Woodrow Wilson would not stand for such impudence and sent the U.S. Army to save the day. But Villa and his band proved elusive, so American General John Joseph "Black Jack" Pershing stabled the horses his soldiers had been riding and sent out a call for motorcycles.

On March 16, 1916, the U.S. War Department telegraphed the Harley-Davidson Motor Company requesting that a dozen motorcycles be shipped immediately to Fort Sam Houston, Texas. They arrived two days later, ready for action and equipped with William S. Harley's latest creation: sidecars mounted with armored Colt machine guns. Pershing and his motorized cavalry chased Villa and his banditos away from Texas and into the deserts of northern Mexico.

Maintaining your Harley-Davidson
The Motor Company provided everything you needed to keep your Harley-Davidson running, from instruction books to parts, tools to a Service School. For identification of the pictured items, see page 114. *Doug Leikala collection.*

This first use of the Harley-Davidson in a military campaign taught the army the value of motorcycles and motorized troops—and taught the army that it had no means of maintaining these new marvels. Once again, the Motor Company stepped in to fill the gap, establishing its Service School in 1917 to train military personnel to repair and maintain its motorcycles. After the end of the war to end all wars, World War I, the Service School was expanded to provide education for dealers and their mechanics, passing on the school's hard-won expertise.

The motorcycle had been born of tinkerers and inventors, and it required tinkerers and inventors to keep motorcycles alive. William S. Harley, Arthur Davidson, and the rest of the Davidson clan were all tinkerers and inventors. After crafting a motorcycle in a shed, they also had to learn how to tame and care for their creation. This was a key reason that the fledgling Harley-Davidson company eschewed racing for its first decade, choosing instead to concentrate on developing and refining its motorcycle. This dedica-tion paid off, as Walter Davidson himself proved when he and his single-cylinder Harley-Davidson won the 1908 Federation of American Motorcyclist endurance and reliability contest with a perfect score.

Within a few years, to ensure that this reputation for reliability endured, the Motor Company began to train its dealers and their mechanics through the Service School. Harley-Davidson also provided owners with rider's handbooks full of advice on the care and feeding of their motorcycle. Over the years, many owners' mechanical aptitudes may have been at a level where they must have aspired to *become* shade-tree mechanics while harboring faith in baling wire and hammers to cure what ailed their motorcycles. But throughout, Harley-Davidson stood by, providing everything from oil to lubricate the interior of the motor to Gunk degreaser to clean the spent oil off the exterior of the motor, as well as various and sundry tools, spare parts, and touch-up paints to help fuel the passion.

Literature

Facing page: Harley-Davidson was a prolific publisher, sending out brochures, rider's handbooks, dealer news, and its famous owner's magazine, *The Enthusiast*. Owner's clubs added to the paper piling up on an owner's desk; this club news magazine, *Entusiasten*, is from the Harley Davidson Club Sweden. *Dudley Perkins Harley-Davidson collection.*

Maintenance memorabilia
Identification of the maintenance items on page 112: 1. Gunk motorcycle cleaner, 1950s; 2. Oil can, 1940s; 3. Tool kit, 1910s; 4. Rider's handbooks and maintenance guides from the 1930s through the 1970s; 5. Spark plug, 1930s; 6. Quick-drying enamel paint, 1960s; 7. Spark plug, 1970s; 8. Oil ad, 1940s; 9. Gunk ad, 1950s; 10. Harley-Davidson tools, 1940s and 1950s; 11. Chain grease, 1930s.

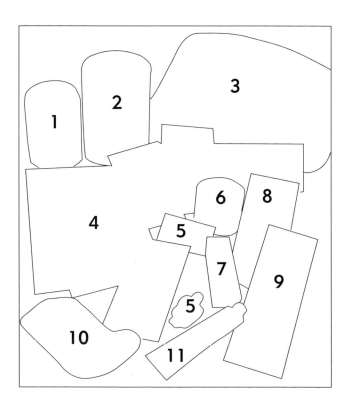

Dealership parts counter, 1947

Karl's Cycles in Minneapolis, Minnesota, was a landmark for Harley-Davidson riders for decades. This view of the parts counter, with Karl Hechrich himself at center, shows the typical 1940s dealership, well stocked with official Motor Company parts and cans of Genuine Harley-Davidson Oil. The two youngsters were probably your typical shop rats, enthusiasts in the making. *Minnesota Historical Society collection.*

Running and adjusting instructions, 1941
As these pamphlets warned, "Trouble-free performance and low maintenance cost are not matters of good or bad luck." These running and adjusting instructions covered the 61-cubic-inch (1,000-cc) overhead-valve Knucklehead (left) and the 74- and 80-cubic-inch (1,200- and 1,300-cc) side-valves. *Dudley Perkins Harley-Davidson collection.*

Oil cans, 1950s, 1940s, and 1930s
The Motor Company recommended owners use only "Genuine" motor oil, available from your local Harley-Davidson dealer. Over the years, there were numerous small variations in container types, even though they used the same logo; some have slight text variations but may be close in vintage. Early one-quart (0.9-liter) containers may be made of metal or paper. *Chris Haynes collection.*

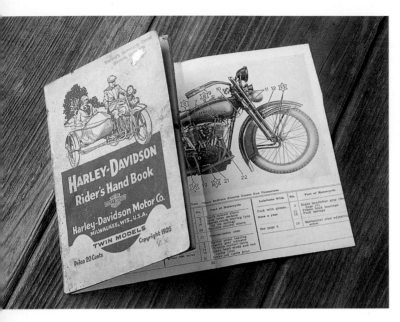

Rider's handbook, 1926

Above: The Motor Company always provided new owners with a rider's handbook that detailed how to maintain, ride, and lubricate the motorcycle. Harley-Davidson naturally had a vested interest in maintaining its motorcycle, and thus maintaining its reputation for reliability. *Mike Parti collection.*

1929 Model B

Right: Harley-Davidson started with single-cylinder motorcycles, and even though the V-twins became the company's flagship line, it continued to produce and sell singles up through 1934. The Model A, B, AA, and BB lines were introduced in 1926 with the side-valve A and B churning out 8 hp from their 21.10-cubic-inch (345-cc) engines while the AA and BB featured overhead valves and 10 hp. The B and BB boasted battery ignition and lighting. Owner: David Patrick.

Oil cans, 1960s

An assortment of 1960s Harley-Davidson oil cans. *Chris Haynes collection.*

Racing oil can, 1960s

A can of Harley-Davidson racing motor oil. *Chris Haynes collection.*

Oil can, 1950s

A one-gallon (3.8-liter) can of Harley-Davidson Pre-Luxe oil. *Chris Haynes collection.*

Fluids

The Motor Company sold all of the fluids a Harley-Davidson owner would need for his or her motorcycle—except gasoline. *Dudley Perkins Harley-Davidson collection.*

Tools, 1930s

A Harley-Davidson grease gun (top) and chain tool. *Paul Wheeler collection.*

Knucklehead and service items, 1930s–1970s

Above: An array of Harley-Davidson's service parts, oils, and other maintenance fluids surround one of the Motor Company's finest. *Vince Spadaro collection.*

Tools, 1930s through 1990s

Left: Harley-Davidson offered standard tool kits to owners, as well as specialized tools, through the accessory catalog. *Chris Haynes collection.*

1970 XLH

Sportsters were running strong in the 1970s when this electric-start XLH was built. The fiberglass "Boattail" seat-and-fender unit was optional, and most buyers opted for the standard seat. Owner: Mike Quinn.

Oil cans, 1970s
Premium and Pre-Luxe cans of Harley-Davidson motor oil from the 1970s. *Chris Haynes collection.*

Oil cans, 1970s
Premium and Pre-Luxe cans of Harley-Davidson motor oil from the 1970s. *Chris Haynes collection.*

Gas additives, 1950s and 1960s
Above: Two jars of Harley-Davidson gasoline additive. *Threedouble collection.*

Gunk cans, 1950s through 1970s
Right, top: Three styles and sizes of Gunk cans dating from the 1950s (left), 1960s (center), and 1970s. *Chris Haynes collection.*

Cylinder coating, 1940s
Right, center: A can of black cylinder coating to help in keeping up appearances. *Threedouble collection.*

Lube oil, 1950s
Right, bottom: A handy tube of lube oil with a welcome to your local Harley-Davidson dealership. *Threedouble collection.*

Gunk sign, 1950s
Above: The Motor Company sold its Gunk motorcycle cleaner to owners through the decades. This plastic dealer sign would have been placed in a prominent position on a parts counter. *Doug Leikala collection.*

Gunk cans
Left: Two one-gallon (3.8-liter) cans of Gunk cleaner. *Chris Haynes collection.*

Spark plug, 1937
Above: This special U.S. government box states, "1-PLUG, spark w/GASKET (No. 3)." *Mike Parti collection.*

Fluids and parts, 1930s through 1960s
Right, top: A selection of Harley-Davidson fluids and spare parts dating from the 1930s through the 1960s. *Threedouble collection.*

Bearings, 1937
Right, bottom: A Harley-Davidson bearings race with original box. *Paul Wheeler collection.*

Spark plug, 1930s–1940s
Left: A Harley-Davidson wide-body spark plug with original box. Used originally in 1930s and 1940s motorcycles, these plugs continued to be sold by Motor Company dealerships through the 1950s. *Paul Wheeler collection.*

Battery display, 1950s
Above: A Harley-Davidson battery display stand with built-in charging unit. *Vince Spadaro collection.*

Battery, 1970s
Left: A Harley-Davidson "Tar Top" battery used from 1929 through the 1980s. *Chris Haynes collection.*

Dealer shop sign, 1980s

Above: Among other items, this 1980s shop sign noted (farcically) that "I buy junk and sell fine used parts/I cheat drunks and tourists." The shop also quotes their standard rates for customers who want to watch or, for twice the price, help. *Chris Haynes collection.*

Fluid containers, 1980s

Left, top: Four types of 1980s fluids in plastic containers. *Chris Haynes collection.*

Oil containers, 1990s

Left: Three types of 1990s plastic oil containers. *Chris Haynes collection.*

1988 XL 883
In the 1980s and 1990s, Sportsters have won a well-deserved cult following. They're quick, inexpensive, and stylish, and the ideal entry to the Harley-Davidson world. Owner: John Van Dyke.

Spare parts

Above: A selection of Harley-Davidson parts boxes from the 1940s through the 1970s showing the changes in graphic styles. *Chris Haynes collection.*

Paint cans

Right: Five styles of cans, from the 1950s through the 1970s, of Harley-Davidson quick-drying and heat-resistant enamel paint. *Chris Haynes collection.*

Touch-up paints
Above, top: A selection of touch-up paints from the 1950s through the 1970s. *Threedouble collection.*

Touch-up spray paints, 1960s and 1970s
Above, bottom: Three cans of Harley-Davidson spray paints. *Chris Haynes collection.*

Touch-up paint, 1930s
Left, top: A can of quick-drying black enamel "put up by" Harley-Davidson. *Chris Haynes collection.*

Touch-up paints, 1950s
Left, bottom: Harley-Davidson touch-up paints from the 1950s in four original colors. *Threedouble collection.*

Chapter 6

Dressed *for* Success

Harley-Davidson Accessories, Ornaments, & Custom Parts

To many owners, the Harley-Davidson motorcycle as it comes new from the factory is simply a place to begin, a blank canvas on which to work their art. Some owners dress their Harley-Davidsons to the nines with saddle bags, windshields, and touring accessories to be prepared for anything on the open road. Others strip down their pride and joy to the essentials—bob the fenders, hop up the engine, and ditch the stock mufflers, replacing them with straight pipes to create lightweight, high-performance street machines. Still others customize their cycles, chop them, stretch them, lower them, and more.

The Motor Company long supplied optional parts for its motorcycles, primarily through the pages of its accessory catalogs. Today, these catalogs and the accessory equipment they offered provide insight into the styles of different eras of motorcycling. To the motorcycle enthusiast, mechanical parts are things of beauty, and a simple shifter knob—whether it is a 1930s dice knob, a 1940s onyx knob with a Scottie dog, or an immaculately polished chrome knob from the 1950s—tells volumes, evoking a time and place in the past.

Accessories
The Harley-Davidson motorcycle as it came from the dealer's showroom is a blank canvas for owners to work their art on. For identification of the pictured items, see page 134. *Doug Leikala collection.*

Accessory catalogs of the 1920s offered items that riders of today consider necessities, items such as headlamps and taillights, speedometers, and horns. By the 1940s, the accessory catalog offered a wide assortment of optional parts that ranged from valuable riding equipment to ornamental dresser items. On the necessity side, the 1941 catalog displayed everything from wind- and legshields to fringed and bejeweled Buddy Seats, steering dampers to the Jiffy Stand kickstand. For ornamental accessories, there were chrome-plated, flexible "stacks" for exhaust pipes; reflector "jewels"; handlebar-mounted memo pad holders; license plate frames; and enough extra lamps to light up the night, including fog lenses, parking lights, marker lights, fender lamps, and brake lights.

Following on the heels of the first screening of *Easy Rider*, the chopper craze of the 1970s, and the rise of competing accessory parts suppliers such as Custom Chrome and Drag Specialties, the Motor Company inaugurated its own line of Screamin' Eagle high-performance parts and Motor Accessories customizing parts. The Screamin' Eagle line includes everything from hotter cams to trick ignition systems; Motor Accessories run the gamut from windshields to stylish mufflers.

Styles in motorcycles—as with styles of clothes and cars—come and go. In the end, beauty is in the eye of the beholder.

Accessories

Identification of the accessories on page 132: 1. Airplane fender ornament, 1950s; 2. Kidney belt, 1940s; 3. Sheepskin-lined rider's hat, 1950s; 4. Fire extinguisher, 1940s; 5. Nickel spots for saddle bags, 1950s; 6. Eagle fender ornament, 1930s; 7. Top plate, 1930s; 8. Red handlebar grip, 1950s; 9. Accessory catalog, 1912; 10. Pocket watch, 1910s; 11. Dice shifter knob, 1930s; 12. Dice-topped keys, 1930s; 13. Accessory advertisements, 1950s and 1960s; 14. Odometer, 1910s.

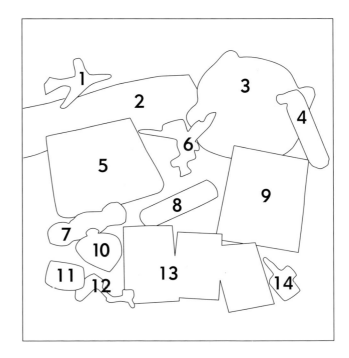

Pogostick accessory, 1912
A Harley-Davidson accessory that never was: This cartoon from a 1912 issue of *Motorcycle Illustrated* magazine details the benefits of the Spring Hopper attachment for motorcycles. *Michael Dregni collection.*

Windshield, 1960s
This new-old-stock 1960s windshield is still in its original box. *Vince Spadaro collection.*

Commemorative gas tank, 1976
To celebrate the United States bicentennial, Harley-Davidson offered this commemorative gas tank, an amazing example of 1970s artwork. *Paul Wheeler collection.*

Accessory catalogs, 1972 and 1973
Fashions and fads of the 1970s filled the covers and pages of these two AMF-era accessory catalogs. *Chris Haynes collection.*

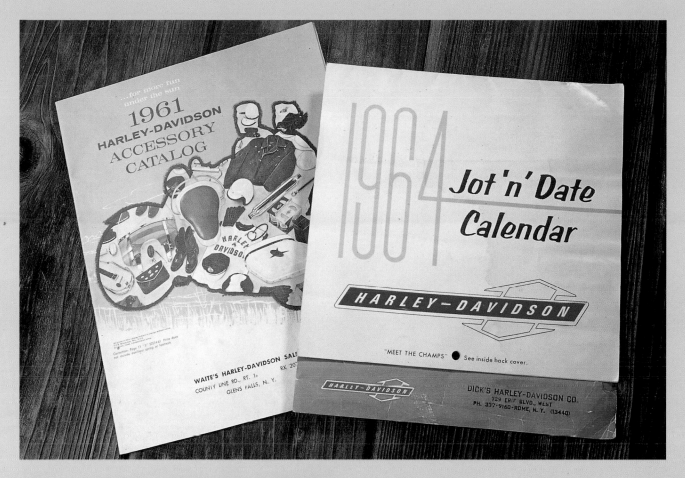

Accessory catalog and calendar, 1960s

Above: The 1961 accessory catalog (left) offered the consummate rider everything from leather jackets to saddle bags. The 1964 Jot'n'Date calendar invited you to "Meet the Champs"—Harley-Davidson's pin-up motorcycles of the year. *Chris Haynes collection.*

Accessory catalog, 1950

Left: Harley-Davidson's accessory catalogs read like a wish list of riding clothes, tools, and shop supplies for the proud new owner. As with the titling of its owner magazine, the Motor Company was inconsistent in its name for the accessory catalog: It was often officially titled simply *Accessory Catalog*, the name it is commonly referred to by; at other times it was titled *Harley-Davidson Motorcycling Accessories*, *Accessories for Your Motorcycle*, and other names. This 1950 accessory catalog boasted of "America's Most Complete Line of Motorcycle Accessories." *Threedouble collection.*

Michigan. In 1914 in Cleveland, Ohio, the first traffic light in the United States was erected, featuring buzzers as well as green and red lights, but there was still no uniform traffic controls in North America; some cities had electric stoplights, others had mechanical semaphore arms, others were free-for-alls. Even as late as 1930, sixteen American states had no uniform code for hand signals, and a dozen had no speed limits whatsoever.

To uphold law and order and control the burgeoning ranks of automobiles, motorcycles, and electric streetcars that were soon outnumbering horses and horse-drawn wagons in city traffic around the turn of the century, police forces needed help. Philadelphia, Pennsylvania, was the first city in North America to inaugurate a police traffic squad, in 1904; it was followed by New York City in 1907. Yet the motorized perpetrators could easily outrun or outdistance the traffic police who were on foot or horseback. In 1902, the Boston, Massachusetts, police force bought a Stanley Steamer, believed to be the first police automobile in North America; in 1903, New York City police stepped up from horses to bicycles, but still the traffic violators eluded them.

In the days before cars were widely affordable and readily available to police forces, motorcycles proved to be the answer. According to Motor Company lore as reported in *The Harley-Davidson Enthusiast* in 1916, the first Harley-Davidson in uniform was inducted into the Pittsburgh, Pennsylvania, police force, in 1909.

In 1916, Harley-Davidsons were enlisted to patrol the U.S.–Mexico border after the Mexican Revolution and the resulting instability, soon proving their utility and reliability. When World War I flared, the U.S. Army was well equipped with Motor Company motorcycles: Some 26,486 Harley-Davidsons saw service, according to U.S. War Department records. The American armed services continued to use Harley-Davidsons in World War II, inspiring the WLC model for the Canadian Army, the short-lived XA prototype, and the WLA for the U.S. Army and other forces around the globe.

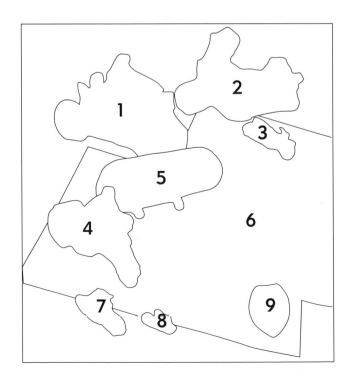

Police memorabilia
Identification of the police collectibles on page 146: 1. Cast-iron police sidecar rig; 2. Police model; 3. Police toy motorcycle; 4. Hubley cast-iron police sidecar rig, 1930s; 5. Police fender plate, 1920s; 6. Harley-Davidson police model literature, 1950s and 1960s; 7. Police toy; 8. Police toy; 9. Motorcycle police badge, 1950s.

Police literature, 1953

Police business was big business for the Motor Company. Harley-Davidson's Public Safety Division kept officers of the law informed about late breaking news in the motorcycle world. *Doug Leikala collection.*

Police literature, 1953

Far left: Police flyers and promotional posters designed to woo the men and women in blue to take up Harley-Davidson. *Doug Leikala collection.*

Police literature, 1955

Left: "Stop speeding and road hogging before it starts." Harley-Davidson literature played to the police officer's sympathies in these 1955 brochures. *Doug Leikala collection.*

Police helmet, 1960s
Above: A Traffic Officer helmet from the Los Angeles Police Department. *Paul Wheeler collection.*

Police equipment, 1960s
Right: This police fender sign and speedometer—emblazoned with the words "Police Special"—date from the late 1960s. *Doug Leikala collection.*

Police ledger books, 1920s through 1950s
Right, top: The Motor Company provided police motorcycle units with ledger notebooks throughout the years. *Doug Leikala collection.*

Police banner
Right, bottom: This banner once flew from a motorcycle patrol's mount. *Threedouble collection.*

Police humor, 1940s and 1950s
Below: *Doug Leikala collection.*

Police sirens, 1940s and 1950s
Above: A selection of 1940s and 1950s Harley-Davidson police sirens. *Paul Wheeler collection.*

Police siren, 1960s
Right: A 1960s Harley-Davidson police siren. *Paul Wheeler collection.*

Parking enforcement team, 1950s
Above: Two parking enforcement officers stand proudly alongside their 1950s Servi-car. *Michael Dregni collection.*

Parking patrol chalk, 1940s
Above right: Harley-Davidson thought of everything: As the box said, "Chalk For Car Marking Stick." *Mike Parti collection.*

Police badge, 1950s
Left: A motorcycle police badge from an unspecified American force. *Threedouble collection.*

Police toys, 1950s

Everything Junior and Sis needed to transform themselves into Motorcycle Junior Police—everything that is, except a Harley-Davidson. As the identification card stated, "This is to certify that the undersigned is a member of the Juvenile Police Force, and will uphold the law to the best of his ability." *Doug Leikala collection.*

Toy handcuffs, 1950s
Above: *Threedouble collection.*

Crime Buster Police Badge, 1960s
Right: *Threedouble collection.*

Whistle, 1950s
Left: A toy whistle featuring a police officer on his mount. The plastic whistle was made by Commonwealth Plastics Corporation in the United States in the 1950s. *Threedouble collection.*

Annotated
Bibliography

In addition to consulting numerous Harley-Davidson general model catalogs, accessory catalogs, MotorClothes catalogs, and various issues of *The Enthusiast*, the following books were consulted and are recommended:

Harley-Davidson and General Motorcycle Collectibles

Dunbar, Leila. *Motorcycle Collectibles*. Atglen, Pa.: Schiffer Publishing, 1996.
An identification and price guide to a wide variety of American motorcycle collectibles with numerous color photographs. The memorabilia comes primarily from the author's own collection as well as those of Doug Leikala and Cris and Pat Simmons, with individual items from other collectors. Includes a substantial chapter on motorcycle miniatures, primarily made by Hubley.

Dregni, Michael, and Eric Dregni. *Scooters!* Osceola, Wis.: Motorbooks International, 1995.
A history of the motorscooter with historical photographs, collectibles, and memorabilia.

Mitchel, Doug. *Harley-Davidson Chronicle: An American Original*. Lincolnwood, Ill.: Publications International, 1996.
A large, detailed photographic history of Harley-Davidson motorcycles including motorcycle toys (most of which are not Harley-Davidson models), memorabilia, and collectibles.

Rafferty, Tod. *Harley Memorabilia: An Illustrated Guide to Harley-Davidson Collectibles, Keepsakes and Mementos*. Edison, N.J.: Chartwell Books, 1997.
An excellent illustrated price guide to Harley-Davidson collectibles by a respected Harley historian.

Motorcycle Toys

Gottschalk, Lillian. *American Motortoys*. London: New Cavendish Books, 1986.
A stunning art book focusing primarily on toy cars but including some motorcycles and providing brief histories of the major toy makers.

Longest, David. *Antique & Collectible Toys 1870–1950: Identification & Values*. Paducah, Ky.: Collector Books, n.d.
While this book covers all sorts of toys, it does have a good, yet short, chapter on transportation toys.

Gibson-Downs, Sally, and Christine Gentry. *Motorcycle Toys: Antique and Contemporary, Identification & Values*. Paducah, Ky.: Collector Books, n.d.
An encyclopedic guide to motorcycle toys with chapters on early cast-iron and pressed-metal toys. Unfortunately, more than half of the book is devoted to contemporary die-cast toys, action figures, and hobby kits that are of little interest to most collectors. Nevertheless, it is still the best reference currently available.

Mostra del Giocattolo d'Epoca e sua Cultura. Florence: Mostra Mercato Internazionale dell'Antiquariato di Firenze, 1989.
2ª Mostra del Giocattolo d'Epoca e sua Cultura. Florence: Mostra Mercato Internazionale dell'Antiquariato di Firenze, 1991.
These two Italian-language catalogs are survey histories of European toys of all sorts, but include many

photographs of Italian, Spanish, French, and German motorcycle and scooter toys.

O'Brien, Richard. *Collecting Toys: Identification and Value Guide*, 8th ed. Iola, Wis.: Krause Publications, 1997. This guide is encyclopedic in covering all types of toys and includes a substantial section on automotive and motorcycle miniatures.

Harley-Davidson History

Bolfert, Thomas C. *The Big Book of Harley-Davidson*, rev. ed. Milwaukee, Wis.: Harley-Davidson, 1991. A fun scrapbook of Motor Company history with many archival photographs and ads that only Tom Bolfert, director of advertising for Harley-Davidson's Parts and Accessories division, could find.

Field, Greg. *Harley-Davidson Knuckleheads*. Osceola, Wis.: Motorbooks International, 1997. An amazing book of Harley-Davidson history focusing on a pivotal model. The book reads like a technical thriller and is packed with detailed text, photographs, and captions.

Field, Greg. *Harley-Davidson Panheads*. Osceola, Wis.: Motorbooks International, 1995. Another excellent book devoted to a single Harley-Davidson model, again packed with detailed text, photographs, and captions.

Girdler, Allan. *The Harley-Davidson and Indian Wars*. Osceola, Wis.: Motorbooks International, 1997. An innovative look at the often contentious history of the two major American motorcycle makers and how they battled each other on the showroom floors, on the racetracks, and for the enthusiast's loyalty. Allan Girdler is one of the most insightful and entertaining writers on motorcycles around.

Hatfield, Jerry. *Illustrated Antique American Motorcycle Buyer's Guide: 1903[sic]–1936 From Ace to Yale*. Osceola, Wis.: Motorbooks International, 1996. Jerry Hatfield is one of the foremost historians of the American motorcycle, and this book is a masterful survey of American motorcycles from the first Indian prototype of 1901 and covers all makes including Harley-Davidson, Excelsior, Henderson, and the numerous orphan makers and models.

Hatfield, Jerry. *Inside Harley-Davidson: An Engineering History of the Motor Company from F-Heads to Knuckleheads 1903–1945*. Osceola, Wis.: Motorbooks International, 1990. This is one of Hatfield's best books, providing a wealth of development and technical detail, dispelling some myths, and uncovering much new data.

Palmer, Bruce III. *How to Restore Your Harley-Davidson*. Osceola, Wis.: Motorbooks International, 1994. The appendices to this mammoth book include an excellent listing of colors, equipment groups, and some accessories for 1937–1964 V-twins.

Motoring History

Automobile Manufacturers Association. *A Chronicle of the Automotive Industry in America*. Detroit, Mich.: Automobile Manufacturers Association, [1949].

Finch, Christopher. *Highways to Heaven: The Auto Biography of America*. New York: HarperCollins, 1992.

McShane, Clay. *Down the Asphalt Path: The Automobile and the American City*. New York: Columbia University Press, 1994.

Guitar History

Smith, Richard R. *Fender Custom Shop Guitar Gallery*. Milwaukee, Wis.: Hal Leonard Corp., 1996. This stylish look inside Fender's Custom Shop, published in cooperation with Fender, features breathtaking photography by the Pitkin Studio. Several pages—including a gatefold spread—are devoted to the Harley-Davidson guitar.

Index

About the photographer and author

Nick Cedar is a long-time fan of vintage motorcycles, and has been photographing them for twelve years for publications such as *Iron Works*, *Motorcycle Collector*, and *American Motorcyclist*. His work has been published in numerous other magazines, books, and calendars as well.

He received a BFA in photography at the Academy of Arts College in San Francisco, and he lives in northern California with his wife, Kris, and his two cats, Rufus and Betisse. He is currently saving his pennies for a 1966 FLH or Sportster.

Photograph by Kris Dickinson

Michael Dregni first fell in love with motorcycles as a child. He is the author of *Inside Ferrari*, an engineering history of Ferrari automobiles, and co-author of two pop culture histories of motorscooters, *Scooters!* and *Illustrated MotorScooter Buyer's Guide*. He is currently working with Bruno Baccari on a history of Parilla motorcycles to be published in Italy. He lives in Minneapolis, Minnesota, with his wife Sigrid, son Nico, dog Ciccia, and more motorcycles than he dares to count.

Photograph by Sigrid Arnott